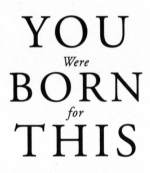

YOU
Were
BORN
for
THIS

BRUCE WILKINSON

Author of the *New York Times* #1 Bestseller *The Prayer of Jabez*
with DAVID KOPP

YOU *Were* BORN *for* THIS

7 Keys to a Life of Predictable Miracles

MULTNOMAH
BOOKS

You Were Born for This
Published by Multnomah Books
12265 Oracle Boulevard, Suite 200
Colorado Springs, Colorado 80921

Every story in this book is an account of an actual event. No composite anecdotes or other fiction techniques have been used. However, details in some stories have been modified slightly to improve readability or to protect privacy.

ISBN 978-1-60142-182-1
ISBN 978-1-60142-184-5 (electronic)

Published in the United States by WaterBrook Multnomah, an imprint of the Crown Publishing Group, a division of Random House Inc., New York.

MULTNOMAH and its mountain colophon are registered trademarks of Random House Inc.

Library of Congress Cataloging-in-Publication Data
Wilkinson, Bruce.
    You were born for this : seven keys to a life of predictable miracles / Bruce Wilkinson ; with David Kopp.
— 1st ed.
        p. cm.
    Includes bibliographical references.
    ISBN 978-1-60142-182-1 — ISBN 978-1-60142-184-5 (electronic)
    1. Miracles. 2. Christian life. I. Kopp, David, 1949- II. Title.
    BV4509.5.W4835 2009
    234'.13—dc22

                                    2009028443

Printed in the United States of America
2009—First Edition

10 9 8 7 6 5 4 3 2 1

SPECIAL SALES
Most WaterBrook Multnomah books are available at special quantity discounts when purchased in bulk by corporations, organizations, and special-interest groups. Custom imprinting or excerpting can also be done to fit special needs. For information, please e-mail SpecialMarkets@WaterBrookMultnomah.com or call 1-800-603-7051.

DEDICATION

—❧—

To Him who is able to do exceedingly abundantly
above all that we ask or think,
according to the power that works in us, to Him be glory.

from Ephesians 3:20–21

Contents

PART 1: WELCOME TO EVERYDAY MIRACLE TERRITORY

1. A New Way to See the World 3
   You were born to expect a miracle today

2. The Tiny, Enormous Difference 19
   You were born to do God's work by God's power

3. Behind the Veil of Heaven 35
   You were born to be a living link between Heaven and earth

PART 2: FOUR KEYS TO A LIFE OF MIRACLES

Introduction to the Miracle Life Keys 49

4. The Master Key 53
   You were born to be sent on miracle missions

5. The People Key 65
   You were born to share God's heart for people

6. The Spirit Key 79
   You were born to partner with God's Spirit

7. The Risk Key 93
   You were born to take risks of faith in dependence on God

PART 3: HOW TO DELIVER A MIRACLE

8. The Five Signals That Guide a Miracle Delivery 107
   You were born to understand and respond to miracle-related signals

9. The Five Steps That Lead to a Miracle Delivery 131
You were born to know and follow miracle-related delivery steps

PART 4: THREE KEYS TO SPECIAL DELIVERY MIRACLES

Introduction to the Special Delivery Keys 149

10. The Money Key 153
You were born to deliver miracles of financial provision

11. The Dream Key 171
You were born to deliver miracles of life purpose

12. The Forgiveness Key 193
You were born to deliver miracles of forgiveness

Epilogue: Welcome to the Beginning 213

Acknowledgments 223
Appendix: 15 Frequently Asked Questions About
the Miracle Life 225
Notes 226

Part 1

WELCOME TO EVERYDAY MIRACLE TERRITORY

1

A New Way to See the World

You were born to expect a miracle today

What if I told you I'm certain you missed a miracle yesterday? And not just any miracle but one that Heaven wanted to do through you to significantly change someone's life for the better—maybe your own?

I would understand if you were doubtful.

But right alongside that doubt, most of us can identify a nearly universal experience. Almost everyone in the world—whatever their religious belief—can point to an event in their lives that seemed directly orchestrated by Heaven, that seemed impossible to explain without using words like "I can't believe what just happened! That was a miracle!" We call these experiences divine coincidences, miracle moments, supernatural provisions. Whatever we call them, we tend to value such events so highly that we recount them over and over, often for years. "I'll never forget the time…," we say, or "Sooner or later my daughter is going to tell you about…"

Why do we remember such events so clearly? I think it's because we feel that we have been touched by Heaven. It's as if God Himself stepped through the curtain that separates the seen from the unseen to make something wonderful happen for us, something only He could do.

But here's the best part. In the experience we hear a personal and unforgettable message from God. Something like, *I'm here. I care about you. I can do for you what you cannot do for yourself.*

Beginning with this near-universal experience, this book asks a few simple but intriguing questions:

- Why are these experiences of the miraculous so rare for most people?
- What if Heaven actually wanted you to experience them on a regular basis?
- What if ordinary people like you and me are invited to partner with God to deliver miracles to others?

If these questions put a picture in your mind of people everywhere walking around expecting to be a part of miracle moments on a regular basis, you're not far wrong.

A mysterious encounter

Let me tell you about a mysterious encounter I had in a restaurant outside Denver with a waiter named Jack. I call it mysterious because on the surface everything looked so ordinary. Five friends at a table for six, waiters coming and going, voices, clatter—just what you'd expect in a busy restaurant. But by the time dinner was over, we all knew beyond a doubt that we'd been present for a divine appointment.

It was as if God Himself had walked up and said, "Thank you for saving Me a place. I've been wanting to do something for Jack."

Here's what happened.

During the course of the meal, Jack had served us well. But apart from the usual exchanges about the menu and our orders, we hadn't spoken much. Around the table, meanwhile, the conversation revolved around some of Jesus' more extreme teachings—ones like "Ask, and you will receive" and "It is more blessed to give than to receive." During the conversation I felt unexpectedly nudged by Heaven to try something I'd never done before. At the same time I sensed it was meant to involve Jack.

My experiment involved putting three hundred dollars "at risk." Now, don't let the amount throw you. The money wasn't mine, and believe it or not, the person who was letting me carry it around was expecting me to give it away. (But more about that in a later chapter.)

When Jack came by to refill the water glasses, I posed a question. "Have you ever heard the saying 'It is more blessed to give than to receive'?"

"Yes, I have," he said.

"Do you believe that?"

"Sure, I guess I do," he said, looking puzzled.

"Good!" I said. "I have an interesting opportunity for you." I placed a hundred-dollar bill on the table. "You have an unusual choice, Jack. You can either receive this hundred dollars as a gift, not a tip…"

I paused. I definitely had Jack's attention, and the two couples with me didn't appear to be breathing.

I looked at Jack. "Or you can say no to the money and instead give each of us a dessert. But this would be *you* buying the desserts, not the restaurant. You can't do both things, and there's no right or wrong. So what would you like to do—give or receive?"

Jack just stood there holding the water pitcher. He asked twice if I was serious. Then finally he said, "I'll take the hundred dollars."

True to my word, I handed him the bill.

"Thank you!" he said. Then he walked back to the kitchen.

After he left and my friends started breathing again, we all tried to figure out what had just happened. Was my unusual test about giving and receiving even fair? What was Jack thinking now? And what in the world was he saying to the crew in the kitchen?

All the while I was feeling increasingly uncomfortable. You see, earlier I had slipped another two hundred dollars under my plate. If the waiter had chosen to buy us desserts and not take the hundred—believing that it is more blessed to give than to receive—I was going to give him the hidden two hundred dollars. I had really hoped he would make the self-sacrificial choice because I'd strongly sensed that God wanted to encourage him with the larger sum.

The next time he came around, I said, "I'm curious, Jack. Do you feel like you made the right choice?"

"Absolutely!" he said excitedly. "In fact, it was a miracle. You see, I'm a single dad." He pulled out his wallet and proudly showed us a photo of his three-year-old son. "Isn't he something!" he said with a big smile. Then he explained his reaction. "I have to work three jobs during four days of the week just so I can take care of my son the other three days when my ex-wife works. But I'm having a tough time making ends meet. Just this morning I had to mail my alimony check of a hundred dollars even though my account was down to zero. Driving to work this afternoon, I actually prayed, 'God, please! I need an extra hundred dollars, and I need it tonight!' "

Well, I was speechless, and so were my friends. How could we have known of our waiter's crisis or of his prayer for a hundred dollars?

Then it was my turn to explain. I told him that even if he had decided to give instead of receive, I'd planned to give him the hundred dollars. "But now that I know your story, I agree. You made the right choice."

Suddenly I knew what needed to happen next. "You have to know that none of this money was mine," I told him. "The owner wanted me to pass it on as a kind of message to the right person. And I'm sure that person was you."

I reached under the plate for the other two hundred. "Obviously God wanted you to have the hundred dollars, and He wants you to have this too."

What God thinks is normal

What just happened here? Let's break it down:

- Jack drove to work that evening to wait tables, but he brought with him a secret, pressing need.
- I had come to Colorado from Atlanta on business and ended up having dinner with friends in Jack's restaurant.
- Unbeknown to Jack or my friends, I was prepared to meet someone's financial need with money that wasn't mine.
- By the end of the evening, God had used one person to deliver something that met a big need for another person—and in a way that was clearly miraculous to everyone involved.

You might react differently to what happened around that table. You might think, for example, *Well, I don't have a hundred-dollar bill lying around. And if I did, why would I give it to a stranger? For that matter, how would I figure out whom to give it to?*

We'll look closely at these reactions and more like them in the pages ahead. You'll see, I promise, that God is just as likely to have plans for five dollars or twenty dollars as He is for a hundred dollars and that He never asks you or me to serve Him in a way that doesn't fit us personally and perfectly.

> *God had used one person to deliver something that met a big need for another person—and in a way that was clearly miraculous.*

For now, though, put yourself in the story of our dinner with Jack. Imagine how you would have felt leaving that table and knowing you had played an active role in delivering God's provision for a young man's desperate need. Better yet, imagine a lifestyle of such encounters, where God works through you in unexplainable ways to do a miracle—and on a regular basis.

This kind of life is not only possible but is what God thinks of as normal when He thinks of you.

God did not place you on this earth to notice Him at work only once or twice in your whole life.

You see, He did not place you on this earth to notice Him at work only once or twice in your whole life. He did not create you to consistently miss out on the wonder of His presence and power.

The truth is, you were born to live a supernatural life doing God's work by God's power. You were born to walk out your door each morning believing that God will use you to deliver a necessary miracle today.

This book will show you how.

The Everyday Miracle Territory

When it comes to miracles, most people I know see the world as divided in two.

On the far left is a region we could call the Land of Signs and Wonders. In this land amazing miracles seem to happen a lot, although only for a select few. Mostly this world reveals itself on television, in a few unusual churches, and in faraway places. Still, Signs and Wonders is a remarkable place. In this land the blind regain their sight and invalids throw away their canes to run around like school kids.

On the far right is the Land of Good Deeds. Nobody is putting on a show here. Fortunately, though, the place is full of good people watching out for each other, doing good works. And certainly God is pleased with that.

Interestingly, in Good Deeds land a lot of people believe in miracles and spend time studying them. They just don't expect to actually see any miracles, much less be a part of them on a regular basis. When they praise God for miracles, they're grateful for things that occurred long ago. Good Deeds land doesn't dazzle like Signs and Wonders, but things are more manageable there. More predictable.

What's the one big disadvantage in Good Deeds land? God rarely shows up in a supernatural way. Why would He? No one is expecting the miraculous, and besides, everything is running just fine. Or so it seems.

Which land would you say you live in most of the time?

A large majority of people live in the Land of Good Deeds. Even though some would say they have experienced meaningful personal miracles in the past—at a point of spiritual awakening or in a time of crisis—they believe those experiences are rare. More important, they believe we don't have a role in whether one happens again or not, so there's no point in leaving the house today on the lookout for one.

What I want you to realize is that if you live in either land I've described, you've overlooked the most promising region of all. You see, between the dazzle of Signs and Wonders and the duty of Good Deeds lies a broad and promising middle ground.

In this book we call this in-between land the Everyday Miracle Territory. Here people believe that God wants to intervene—and does—in supernatural ways in human affairs on a regular basis. Here unmet needs are seen by ordinary people as golden opportunities for God to show up, and to do so through them, at almost any moment. They're not waiting for special powers for themselves or for God to part the skies on their behalf. They have experienced miracles and know beyond doubt that miracles are for them and others like them, right here and right now.

Those who live in the Everyday Miracle Territory have already made two startling observations.

One is full of hope. Everywhere they look, in every situation, they see potential for an unforgettable "God-incidence"—not a coincidence but a moment when God steps in to meet a real need through them in a way that only He can. Some days it actually feels as though God has a pile of miracles ready to be delivered!

Their other observation is full of dismay.

They are nearly alone.

Would you agree that few people today are living in Everyday Miracle Territory? I wrote this book to help you see that the land of personal, everyday miracles is your rightful home turf. Instead of focusing on the nature-defying acts that God *is able to* do, this book invites you to encounter the miracles that God *does* do on a regular basis—and to embrace your exciting part in partnering with Him to make them happen.

You'll discover that what God chooses to depend on for these divine encounters is simply a willing servant. No previous experience required. No record of perfection. No special religious gift or qualification. In this book we call these refreshingly ordinary folks "delivery agents" for God. They are men and women who say to Him, "Please send me to do Your work by Your power today!"

That's exactly what Jimmy said.

Jimmy the "delivery guy"

Jimmy is one of the most down-to-earth men I've ever met. He can fix anything, find anything, make do with anything. You're stranded with a handful of folks on a desert island? You want Jimmy in the handful. You want to program your iPhone to walk your dog? Jimmy's your man. Just don't ask him to spend time over tea talking about relationships or contemplating the meaning of the universe.

The first time Jimmy heard that he could cooperate with God in supernatural events on a regular basis, he thought, *Not likely.*

He worked in construction, after all, not ministry. He struggled to come up with even one time in the past ten years when he could say with certainty that the supernatural had clearly showed up. The idea of a lifestyle of miracles felt about as real to Jimmy as taking a road trip through an asteroid belt.

But over the course of a You Were Born for This conference, Jimmy realized that he really did want to learn how to partner with Heaven to do God's work on earth. Taking a big step into the unknown, he committed himself to being God's delivery agent when and where he was called upon.

The next morning, while Jimmy was dropping off windows at a job site, he struck up a conversation with a carpenter named Nick. Nick let it be known that his marriage was on the rocks and that he didn't hold out much hope. He just seemed to want to vent.

Normally Jimmy would have expressed sympathy for a man in that kind of misery, then quickly steered as far away as possible from such a sensitive topic. This time, though, Jimmy hung in there. He listened, identified with Nick's struggle, asked a few questions. Then, sensing that the man's heart was open, he asked a simple but miracle-inviting question he had learned at the conference: "Nick, I really want to help you. What can I do for you?"

Without hesitation the carpenter said, "You could tell me what to do next. I'm tied up in knots, but I really want this marriage to work."

Jimmy panicked. Tell another guy how to fix a relationship? *Not likely!* But he took a deep breath and then took an outrageous step of faith. "Why don't you get something to write with," he told the carpenter, "and when you come back, I'll tell you how to save your marriage."

The truth was, Jimmy was stalling. He didn't have a clue what he was going to tell Nick. But as he explained to me later, he was holding on to a couple of things I had said at the conference: "Relax, the miracle is God's to do, not yours" and "Give God a minute." Something or Someone seemed to be leading the way in this conversation with Nick, and Jimmy was determined to follow.

When the carpenter returned, Jimmy heard himself saying, "You need to go home and make your bed."

Jimmy had no idea where that had come from or what good it was. "That's all I have to say," he told Nick apologetically. "I guess you don't even need to write it down."

But the carpenter was staring at Jimmy with his mouth open.

"How did you know?" he gasped. "That is a giant source of conflict for us! I'm the last one up, and I *never* make the bed. My wife says it's a sign of everything that's wrong with the marriage. I don't get it. But you know what? I'm going to drive back at lunch and make the bed before my wife gets home."

To me, this story demonstrates God's willingness to do a personal miracle if we are willing to deliver one. Nick wasn't expecting help from a stranger. And Jimmy didn't think he had help to give. What he had, though, was a readiness to pass along what God prompted him to say.

But the best thing the story shows is God's heart. He cares about the personal struggles of a carpenter named Nick—and He wanted Nick to see that. He cared enough to show Nick a practical step he could take that might say more to his wife than a love letter and just might turn things around for the couple.

All He needed was Jimmy, delivery agent.

Doing what God wants done

You might be like Jimmy, completely unprepared and unqualified but ready to try something different. You may have grown up in the church and have a long list of religious accomplishments to point to. You may be like Nick, uncertain that God exists or that He cares for you. But Heaven works in ways that seem to apply no matter what our spiritual mind-set happens to be.

Perhaps you've heard about my book *The Prayer of Jabez*. It shows how a little-known prayer from three thousand years ago can still result in great blessing and influence for God in our time. Millions bought the book, prayed the prayer…and were astonished at what God began to do in their lives. One reason the message of that book resonated with so many, I believe, is that it made ministry (which simply means doing what God wants done in the world) accessible as a way of life.

Jabez lived in ancient Israel. The Bible says that he was "more honorable than his brothers," but as far as I can tell, it wasn't because of his superior spiritual status. Perhaps he was "more honorable" because he asked with all his heart for God to do for him and through him exactly what God already wanted to do.

And the Bible says, "God granted him what he requested."[1]

Through the prayer of Jabez, millions learned to ask God to expand their territory of influence for Him and then to put His hand of power on them. Not surprisingly, as soon as they took these brave steps, people started seeing miracle opportunities all over the place. And thousands wrote excitedly to me to report what was happening.

Here's what I want you to see: *The Prayer of Jabez* showed ordinary people how to ask God to greatly expand their opportunities to serve Him. *You Were Born for This* shows ordinary people how to be intentional about and skilled at inviting the miraculous into the midst of that larger life.

Think of *You Were Born for This* as *Jabez* to the miracle power.

For all the Jimmys and Jabezes in the world, this book reveals in practical terms how God works supernaturally through His willing partners to make a difference in people's lives. It's the most rewarding and significant life imaginable!

Wouldn't you know it, in answer to my own prayers during those years, God expanded my territory beyond anything I could have imagined.

He sent our family to Africa.

When good deeds aren't enough

In 2002 my wife, Darlene, and I experienced a clear call to move to Africa to tackle some of the most daunting challenges of our time. "Will you go?" God said to us. "Will you care?"

This was happening during the busiest months of my speaking and writing about Jabez. Why would God ask us to leave behind an exploding ministry based on a book He was so clearly blessing? We didn't understand it.

You might think that someone who has studied the character of God in graduate school and dedicated his life to serving Him wouldn't be surprised when God radically redirects his life. I will confess that until then I had enjoyed a lot of clarity about what God had called me to do. I saw myself as a Bible teacher, leader, and disciple maker. My publisher saw me as an author. And that was that.

But almost overnight we experienced a spiritual awakening to the needs of a continent. Poverty. Prejudice. Hunger. AIDS. Orphans. God seemed to be saying to our family, "My heart breaks over these things. I want your hearts to break over them too."

Without knowing what it might mean, we said yes. Then, believing we had been called to a three- to five-year personal mission, we said good-bye to friends and family and moved to Johannesburg, South Africa.

Good deeds alone will never be enough to meet the desperate needs of our time.

What does this have to do with *You Were Born for This*? From the start we knew that trying to meet any one of those needs would be far too big a task for us. God would have to show up in extraordinary ways or nothing of significance would get done.

And He did. We started not by asking, "What can we do?" but by asking, "What does God want done?" We set some high-risk goals in the areas of greatest need. Our ministry plan expected—even depended on—God to intervene. Finally we set about working with others, including charitable groups, African organizations, government agencies, churches, and thousands of First World volunteers, to meet faith-stretching goals. Of course not everything we tried succeeded. But we kept asking for miracles and taking risks of faith, and God *did* show up, as I'll share in the pages ahead.

By the time we returned to the States, our thinking had changed in two important ways.

First, we'd become convinced that good deeds alone will never be enough to meet the desperate needs of our time. This is true whether the needs are personal or global in scope. We simply need more of God. We desperately need miracles!

Second, we had learned that it's often longtime Christians who resist miracles the most. Many have stopped expecting miracles, asking for them, or even knowing how to partner with God to invite them. In other words, they have abandoned the Everyday Miracle Territory and often measure success by how *little* they need God.

> *You Were Born for This is a bold initiative to reclaim the miraculous as a normal way of life.*

As you'd expect, the consequences of limiting what God does on earth to what we can do for Him are disastrous. Just look around. The most pressing personal and global needs go unmet while a generation asks, "Where is God? Doesn't He care? Does He even exist?"

But it doesn't have to be that way.

Miracles are for everyone

You Were Born for This is a bold initiative to reclaim the miraculous as a normal way of life. Through biblical insights, true stories, and practical how-tos, I'll show you what that new normal could look like for you.

In part 1 you'll see why everyone you encounter has an unmet need that

God strongly desires to meet, very possibly through you. You'll discover that the Everyday Miracle Territory is real—and you're standing in the middle of it.

We define a miracle as "an extraordinary event manifesting divine intervention in human affairs."[2] It's true that most of us will never be empowered by God to heal someone or walk on water. The Bible is clear that not everyone has been gifted to carry out such miracles. Yet the Bible is also clear that we are all invited to do God's work by God's power. That's why in this book we only focus on the personal miracles that are within the reach of all of us.

I'm audacious enough to call these miracles predictable. By that I mean that when we do God's work in God's way, He reveals Himself to be a miracle-working God. I mean that miracles will take place so regularly that their occurrence will seem predictable to you—not because of how or when they occur but because they *will* occur.

In part 2 you'll be introduced to four keys to a life of miracles. They will enable you as a delivery agent for God to

- make a very specific, urgent request;
- understand and accept His miracle agenda for you;
- know how to partner with an unseen power;
- take a promising but life-changing risk.

In part 3 you'll discover practical advice on how to deliver a miracle to someone in need. First you'll learn five universally identifiable signals that will guide you in your partnership with Heaven. Then you'll learn five steps for delivering a miracle. When you learn and apply these truths regularly, you can invite God to do a miracle through you for anyone at any time.

That's a startling statement, isn't it? But as you'll see, God is so intent on meeting people's deepest needs that He is always looking for volunteers who will become living links between Heaven and earth.

In part 4 you'll be introduced to three more keys that unlock what I call special delivery miracles. These miracles meet needs that matter to everyone:

finances, life dreams, and forgiveness. Each chapter is based on surprising insights from the Bible and is illustrated with stories you'll find both instructive and highly motivating.

You Were Born for This will change how you see the world and what you expect God can and will do through you to meet real needs. You will master a few simple but powerful tools and will come to say with confidence, "I want to partner with Heaven to deliver a miracle to someone in need today—and now I know how!"

If that's what you want, I invite you to turn the page.

2

The Tiny, Enormous
Difference

*You were born to do God's work
by God's power*

In the first chapter I described an exciting new life of miracles. And I promised that experiencing the supernatural on a regular basis is the "this" you were born for.

But if waking up to our miracle potential is so wonderful, and if this is what God wants for us, what keeps so many from actually living this way? Why do we continually fall into a rut of trying to help others on our own, of trying to avoid any situation where we would be forced to depend upon God for success?

The truth is, we can be in relationship with God and active in helping others for years without really understanding His ways or allowing Him to work through us in supernatural ways. At the heart of the problem, I believe, is a small distinction with big implications. I'm talking about the difference between knowing about God's power and actually partnering with Him in delivering miracles.

An event in my life illustrates that tiny but enormous difference.

Some years ago I was invited to speak to eighty men at a retreat center. The evening of the event, I asked the person in charge, "What would you like me to do if God shows up tonight?"

He seemed startled. "What do you mean?"

I repeated my question. "If the Lord moves and does something unusual, what do you want me to do?"

He gave it some thought. "Well, it would be important for you to bring things to a close in thirty minutes," he said. "Like we agreed."

"All right," I said. "But if something else occurs that might be unexpected, I'm going to look at you. If you want me to end things, just grab your right ear, and I will close in prayer."

He didn't seem pleased with my backup plan. "I don't need to grab my ear, Dr. Wilkinson. You just close in thirty minutes."

I confess, at this point I imagined God shaking His head in disappointment. You see, I wasn't there only because I'd been invited. Before I'd agreed to come, I'd had a strong sense that I'd already been "sent." (More about that in chapter 4.) Then, as I had prayed about what to say, I'd sensed that Heaven might have something unusual in store.

When the time came, the roomful of men welcomed me warmly, and I launched into my message. No more than five minutes in, I received a divine nudge (more about that later too). In a way that was both unusual and impossible to ignore, my attention was directed toward a man sitting four rows back on the left side of the center aisle.

I decided to trust the nudge—in fact, to risk looking like a fool because of it. I stopped talking, walked down the aisle, and introduced myself. The man's name was Owen. "I sense there is something unusual going on in your life," I told him. "Is there anything I can do for you?"

Alarm was written all over Owen's face. "No!" he exclaimed. "No, not at all. Really, I'm fine."

Now what to do? Nothing but apologize to Owen and get back up front. On the way to the podium, I thought, *Well, Lord, that was unusual.*

You should know, audiences I speak to aren't accustomed to speakers who stop in midsentence and march into the crowd with a point-blank, personal question. (I'm not accustomed to it either, for that matter.) Some men in the room were eying me now as if I might be dangerous.

Once I'd collected my thoughts, I began again. But almost immediately I felt another nudge from God. Same nudge, same man. This time I debated with Heaven, and my case was airtight. *I just did that, Lord, and nothing happened!*

But the nudge was clear. *Go again.*

Have you ever come to a point in your life where you've had to make a choice between everything visible, everything expected and sensible…and something invisible, something inaudible, something known only to you that you can't possibly defend *but that you know in your heart is true*? When God nudged me again, I had one of those moments. My sentences stumbled, then stopped. And I decided to take another risk of faith.

So I picked up a chair from the front, carried it down the aisle, and sat right next to Owen. "Sir, please don't be offended," I said calmly, "but you're not telling the truth."

You could have heard a pin drop.

Owen wore the same look of alarm, but when he finally found his voice, he said, "How on earth did you know?"

"I don't know, really," I said. "But God does, and He has something in mind for you tonight. I sense that something is deeply troubling you."

"The truth is, I'm quitting the ministry tonight," Owen said soberly. "I called my wife this afternoon and told her my decision. Right after your session tonight, I'm done."

We certainly had everyone's attention.

A roomful of witnesses

"Would you mind sharing why you're quitting?" I asked Owen.

Haltingly, Owen told his story. He'd been a successful businessman. But when he felt called by God to work with men, he'd given up his business and put heart and soul into his new ministry. Financially, nothing had gone as expected. "My wife and I have gone broke trying to keep this thing afloat," he said. "We love what we do, but we have lost our savings and our retirement. I've remortgaged our house. My credit cards are maxed out. On top of all that, I'm sixteen thousand dollars in debt..."

Owen was struggling to talk now. "I've had enough," he said quietly. "After tonight, I quit."

Every man in the room could identify with Owen's painful dilemma. If God wanted him to stay in the ministry, why were the circumstances so impossible for him and his family? I said as much to Owen, and I told him that my wife and I had experienced similar testing numerous times.

Then I said, "I have only one question. When you changed course and launched your ministry, was that a career move on your part, or would you say it was in response to a divine call?"

"God called us," he said. "I have no doubt."

"Okay. Would you say that God is now calling you out of the ministry? Is He asking you to leave?"

"No."

"Are you sure you want to leave?"

Owen became agitated. "Well, I'm up to my ears in debt. I *have* to quit! How am I supposed to do this?"

"I understand. But has God asked you to leave?"

A long pause.

"No."

As this little drama played out, the other men listened raptly. And I'd forgotten about the guy in charge who didn't want to have to pull on his ear to get my attention.

"What are you going to do?" I asked Owen.

And then God's Spirit moved into the room—a noticeable awareness that His presence was among us in peace and power. Many in the audience were struggling with their own emotions.

Owen's eyes filled with tears. Then with great effort he said, "I shouldn't quit unless He asks me to leave. I won't quit."

I wanted to test his resolve. "But what about the sixteen-thousand-dollar debt?"

"No, I won't quit." He had decided.

We shook hands on his decision, and when I asked some in the audience to gather around and pray for him, scores of men surrounded him. They poured out their hearts in prayer for Owen. Then we all listened while he prayed an emotional, humble prayer, recommitting himself to his calling.

Men were beginning to filter back to their seats when someone spoke up. "It's not right!" It was the man in charge. "This man is sixteen thousand dollars in debt. My wife and I are going to give him a thousand dollars. What are you going to do?" He looked around the room. He looked at me. "What are *you* going to do? You're the speaker."

I didn't say anything while we all contemplated his challenge. And then, without a word, men started to open their wallets. One by one they walked over to Owen with their gifts. I did too. In no time at all, Owen had sixteen thousand dollars.

Owen was speechless, awestruck by what God had done, and the rest of us were grateful just to have been a part of it. What an unforgettable experience!

Standing beside him in the aisle, I said, "Do you recognize the order of things that just happened? What did you have to decide before God gave you the money?"

"Unless God calls me to, I'm not leaving."

"When you made a decision of loyalty to God," I said, "the powerful arm of God was outstretched from Heaven. Do you recognize who was behind this test?"

"God was. He was testing my loyalty," said Owen.

"How did you do on the test?"

"I almost failed it."

"Yes, but you didn't," I said. "Isn't it interesting that God sent me here on the very night you were going to quit and gave me a supernatural nudge—twice—because He didn't want you to fail the test? And He prompted all these men to meet your need!"

I never got back to my message that night. God clearly had something better in mind. The miracle for Owen was followed by one-on-one miracle breakthroughs for two other men who'd been brought to that room for a reason. But so had all of us. Our paths had been guided there, not for a program, not to hear someone speak, but to be witnesses together of God at work in powerful, personal, and supernatural ways.

I'll admit the whole experience took longer than thirty minutes. But the man in charge never reached for his ear.

A small shift in how we think

How many times do you suppose you have been in a situation where God urgently wanted to do something supernatural—something unexplainable and bigger than you could imagine—but it didn't happen because someone started tugging on his ear?

Maybe that someone was you.

I told the story of the men's retreat at some length because it illustrates the kinds of personal miracles God loves to do and *will* do when He has a willing and responsive delivery agent. The story also shows how a small shift in how we think about the Spirit's power can have enormous, lasting consequences. Consider how close I came to missing out on the miracle God did through me for Owen. How easy it would have been for me to explain away God's nudges and proceed with my talk according to plan. The result would have been a perfectly fine ministry event, but would God's glory and power have been so unforgettably on display? Would Owen's critical need have been met? Not likely.

> *The story shows how a small shift in how we think about the Spirit's power can have enormous consequences.*

So, what made the difference?

Nothing special about me, I assure you. The difference had everything to do with what I know about God's miraculous power, who has access to it, and how it helps us accomplish His work.

As I've traveled the world, I've noticed that many of Christ's followers appear to know a lot about God's Spirit but few understand how practically to partner with Him to bring a personal miracle to another person. I've seen many who long for more of the Spirit and yet resist actively partnering with His power in their lives.

In this chapter I want to help you see some things you might have missed about God's power. I hope you'll see and experience what the men in the room with Owen did that night. The evening awakened them to the hope that ordinary men and women really can actively partner with God to accomplish the miraculous. And they went home determined to be more than witnesses of God at work. They wanted to be agents who know how to deliver His miracles to others.

I wrote this book to awaken that same hope and expectation in you.

We're never more fully alive and complete than when we experience God working through us and in spite of us in a way that changes someone's life right before our eyes. Nothing compares to the wonder of seeing God's goodness and glory break through—and knowing we played a part in it.

Let's begin with what Jesus said about the supernatural power of God.

God in motion

One of the last things Jesus did with His friends before He returned to Heaven was to hand out their new job descriptions. It made for a very short read:

Go into all the world for Me...and do the impossible.

You'll find the complete assignment in Matthew 28:18–20 and Acts 1:4–8, but have you ever wondered how the disciples reacted? I think they might have felt two opposite reactions at the same time. On the one hand, I think they wanted to say, "Please, Lord, no! We can't possibly. Look at our limitations. Look at our failures."

And on the other hand, I think they couldn't wait to get started. They'd already learned a lot from the Master, and His mission for them was glorious beyond words. Why not get right to work?

How would you have reacted?

I want you to see that both of these responses are rooted in the same misunderstanding about how this partnership with Heaven actually works.

Which explains a further instruction Jesus gave His friends:

Wait.[1]

But wait for what? Look at Jesus' explanation of how the impossible would become the norm in the near future:

You shall receive power when the Holy Spirit has come upon you; and you shall be witnesses to Me...to the end of the earth.[2]

The Greek word here for "power" is one that might seem familiar to you—*dynamis.* As you might guess from its English derivations (*dynamite* and *dynamic,* for example), *dynamis* means a certain kind of power. Not potential power, like still air or water, but power in motion. Power like a gale-force wind or Niagara Falls. *Dynamis* means power at work.

When Jesus told His followers to wait for Heaven's dynamis, the message was clear: What I'm sending you to do you cannot do in your own power. You can only do it as My power moves through you.

So wait for it.

The disciples got the message. They waited. And when the Spirit came in power, the world changed. If you've read the stories of the early church in Acts, you know what I mean. Now all believers had the Spirit all the time, not just dwelling in them for renewal and comfort, but working through them to accomplish Heaven's desires for people in need.

What happened next was miraculous.

Imagine the stories told around dinner tables at night.

"Philip, when you followed God's nudge into the desert and that VIP got saved—I'll never forget that!"

"Paul, when you stood up in the town square to talk about Christ and people were throwing rocks, but some people listened and many believed—I'll never forget that!"

"Rhoda, when you shouted, 'Peter is at the door!' even though we were sure he was in prison—I'll never forget that!"

God's power—the dynamis of the Spirit—was at work through them to accomplish what they could never have done on their own.

It's easy to read the accounts of the early church and assume that those were special people living in special days. Some of them had walked with Jesus, after all. Some were apostles. Perhaps that's why many today think they can't expect to partner with the supernatural in similar ways.

But is that assumption true? Listen to one apostle's frank remarks about how much difference being "special" made:

> *I, brethren, when I came to you, did not come with excellence of speech or of wisdom declaring to you the testimony of God.... I was with you in weakness, in fear, and in much trembling. And my speech and my preaching were not with persuasive words of human wisdom, but in demonstration of the Spirit and of power, that your faith should not be in the wisdom of men but in the power of God.*[3]

Weakness, fear, and much trembling? Clearly Paul realized he couldn't achieve ministry success merely by his own effort or ability. But Paul had another stunning insight. He saw that his weakness actually made room—*created a miracle opportunity*—for God to demonstrate His supernatural power.

Let me pull the threads together.

Jesus commissioned every one of His followers—from the original disciples down to you and me—to do for others what we cannot do alone. It is too much for us. But Heaven has released God's dynamis to work in us and through us. Whatever our human limitations, when we know how to partner with Heaven, we will see that *we were born to accomplish by supernatural means what God wants done.*

"Unlock that door, please!"

My first clue that my friend John was a great candidate for miracle missions came when I heard that he was taking the message of *The Prayer of Jabez* to men in jail. In particular, he wanted to teach inmates to be intentional about asking God to supernaturally expand their territory for Him. Only a man who understands the astonishing power of God would attempt such a venture behind bars.

John, a business owner with a big heart, has been visiting men at a local jail for years. "I consider it the most important thing I do all week," he wrote to me. John felt that with God's help he'd been able to do a lot of good for these men. But he wanted to do more. He wanted to do ministry with miracle impact.

What would happen, John wondered, if he taught inmates to be purposeful about inviting God to intervene through them in supernatural ways?

In *The Prayer of Jabez,* I suggest a ministry question: "How may I help you?" Many times in my life this question has led to a miracle opportunity.

"I had no idea how God would use this idea," John wrote. "But the men began to practice asking, 'How may I help you?' You can imagine the jokes flying around. 'Thank you. Would you just unlock that door, please?' "

For reasons John couldn't explain, his class grew from twelve to twenty-seven men. Even behind bars—maybe *because* they were behind bars—the men seemed motivated by the notion that God's power was available to them too. They began taking risks to invite God to work in supernatural ways. Hardened convicts accepted Christ as Savior. A man who'd had continual run-ins with inmates of another ethnicity started to slip encouraging notes under their doors at night.

One day John asked Terrence, a newcomer to the class, "How may I help you?"

Terrence barely hesitated. "I have not seen my child since she was three," he said. "And the child's mother will not communicate with me. She destroys my letters, and I'm afraid my daughter will never know me. The greatest thing for me would be to see my daughter. Can you help with that?"

As he finished, Terrence's eyes filled with tears. And John's heart sank—he didn't have a clue how to help. After talking through several ideas, they both decided that they didn't really have any options.

"We decided the only one who could help was God," recalls John. "So we prayed together. I asked God to intervene for Terrence and to bring his child for a visit."

Terrence agreed to write a letter once more asking the child's mother for a visit. Then they waited to see what God would do.

The following Sunday, when John went back, Terrence hadn't heard a thing—just like all the times before. But what they didn't know then was that his letter had been delivered and the mother and child were already making plans for a visit.

In fact, the very next Sunday, Terrence saw his daughter for the first time in years. He was able to reestablish a relationship with his family, and since that day he has been able to see his daughter regularly.

John's bold experiment in partnering with God for miracles has continued to bring transformation. "Two men received money they weren't expecting. Two other men are organizing full-time ministries for when they are released," says John. "And another guy has made plans to work at a youth camp as part of his rehabilitation."

John has changed too. "I've learned that helping other people to experience personal miracles is the most wonderful encouragement in the world."

What is a personal miracle?

Can you see what separates John's ministry experience from many other kinds of good works for God? It is the same thing, I believe, that set my ministry at the men's retreat apart from a typical, predictably run service.

- We intentionally partnered with God's Spirit—depending on Him for success—in ways that would showcase His character and glory when He met the needs supernaturally.
- We stepped out in faith to do God's work in a context where failure was certain unless He acted.
- We took risks based on our belief that God *wanted* to show up and *would* show up in miraculous ways. And He did.

I use the term *personal miracle* to describe what happens when you help another person by intentionally relying on God's power to meet that individual's need. Why do I call these personal miracles?

First, because the kinds of miracles I'm talking about usually are completed in a person's heart. Even if the miracle itself is evidenced by something tangible—Owen receives sixteen thousand dollars from strangers, Terrence receives a visit from his long-lost daughter—God clearly does a work inside the person's heart as well.

Second, I call these personal miracles because God's purpose for doing any miracle is always the same: to meet a person's need.

And finally, the word *personal* aptly describes the aspect of God's character that is revealed by these kinds of miracles. When God takes the time to intervene in our day to meet a need in a special way that's meaningful to us in particular, we recognize how intimately God knows us and loves us.

A personal miracle is also what the Bible refers to as a good work. But not all good works are miracles. Let me explain.

Most Christians know the importance of expressing their faith through deliberate acts of service to others. Everyone's good works matter a great deal to God. As Paul reminds us, we have been "created in Christ Jesus for good works, which God prepared beforehand that we should walk in them."[4]

But what I want you to see is that good works by your own effort are good and necessary but many times are not enough. And I'm not speaking about our inability to work our way into a saving relationship with God. I mean that among the good works you and I were born to do lies a wide range of accomplishments that are extremely important to God, that we have been commissioned to do for Christ—*and that we absolutely cannot do without His supernatural power working through us.*

Think of the relationship between good works and personal miracles in your life in terms of two equations:

Your good works for God = ministry

Your ministry + God's supernatural power = miracles

For a personal miracle, you must choose to proactively partner with God's supernatural power to do what no good work of your own could. All Christ's followers have been invited into this amazing partnership with Heaven. It's a joint but unequal venture between weak humans and an extraordinary God to pursue His agenda in His way in His time by His power and for His glory.

This amazing partnership changes what we do, how we think, and what we know is possible. We end up deciding it's perfectly natural to expect miracles behind prison bars. We stop in midsentence because God shows us there's a man four rows back on the aisle who feels forgotten by Him.

We're completely prepared to go to the ends of the earth.

Open your eyes

I've noticed that when people start to live every day in active cooperation with the Spirit, something astonishing happens: they immediately recognize the life God intended for them. They see Jesus' promise of dynamis being fulfilled right in front of them, and the difference is so enormous that they wonder how they could have missed it for so long.

But that's the problem. You can be a Christian for years and miss it completely!

I think that explains Paul's unusual concern about this very issue. He described it as an enlightenment problem. You need enlightenment

> *That's the problem. You can be a Christian for years and miss it completely!*

when a fundamental and life-changing truth is just inches away but you can't see it. And if you don't see it, you can't live it. Paul understood that a person can be a true believer in Christ and yet not understand at all how we are to actually accomplish the business of Heaven.

For the believers at Ephesus, he prayed,

> *that...the eyes of your understanding being enlightened* ["enlightened"— there's the key word]; *that you may know* [have a clear mental perception of] *what is...the exceeding greatness of His power* ["power"—that's *dynamis*] *toward us who believe, according to the working of His mighty power* [*dynamis* again] *which He worked in Christ when He raised Him from the dead.*[5]

This is my prayer for you too: that the eyes of your understanding will be enlightened to your miracle potential. If you don't see the truth about God's power, you will come to a sensible but costly conclusion: "I was not born to do God's work by God's power."

Will you see and embrace the truth instead?

It's the difference between life as most people know it and your life as God wants it to be.

It's the difference between a commendable, even God-blessed human endeavor and supernaturally infused life.

It's the difference between your feeling good about what you've done to help others and others feeling astonished by what God has done for them through you.

This book is all about that tiny, enormous difference.

3

Behind the Veil of Heaven

*You were born to be a living link
between Heaven and earth*

If I were to ask you what you think is happening in Heaven at this very moment, what would you say?

I've asked this simple question of religious and nonreligious, educated and uneducated persons the world over. And since most people believe Heaven exists, ideas tend to come quickly.

People mention angels, harps, God sitting on His throne, a lot of praise and worship. Others mention higher states of consciousness. But little involving action comes to mind.

"Any committee meetings going on up there?" I ask. "Strategy planning sessions?"

Folks laugh. They think I'm kidding.

"How about God? Does He do any work? What about God asking for opinions on important matters? Does Heaven have anything like an agenda for the day?"

People don't think so.

I love watching their faces when I ask questions like these. (They do sound a bit far-fetched, don't they?) But the responses I hear are quite revealing. The fact is, most people think God just listens to worship songs. Whenever I ask, "And what does God do when He's finished listening?" all I get is blank stares. To them, Heaven today is nice but not very exciting. It's a place on hold, a celestial waiting room for angels and great-aunts. And whatever does happen there doesn't really affect what happens on earth.

But what if you discovered that the spiritual realm of Heaven and the material realm of earth are actively linked in billions of ways? What if you discovered that God is intently at work right now on tasks that matter greatly to Him and that He's constantly looking for volunteers to help Him?

I want to pull back the veil of Heaven to reveal what God is doing right now to connect with people in need on earth.

We ended chapter 2 with some promises: You were born to deliver miracles for God. You can learn how to partner with Heaven to do God's supernatural work on earth. And it can happen today.

If these possibilities intrigue you, this chapter will show you something astonishing: God wants you to experience a miracle today even more than you do. To show you why that's true, I want to pull back the veil of Heaven to reveal what God is doing right now to connect with people in need on earth.

Snorkel vision

If you've ever snorkeled in tropical waters, you know that if you get it just right, you can see one world through the bottom half of your mask, another through the top. Bottom half—a watery world of coral and colored fish. Top half—sky.

In 1 Kings 22 we get to have a similar experience. One verse shows what's happening on earth. The next verse shows what's happening at the very same time in the courts of Heaven. I think you'll see evidence of a Heaven-earth connection that will revolutionize how you view your world.

What's happening on earth, in this Bible chapter, is a turning point in the history of Israel. A ruthless and corrupt king named Ahab is trying to make a decision. Should he go into battle against Syria or not? His advisors—all of whom worship idols, not God—have told him to march north to battle because victory is guaranteed. But Ahab wavers. He wants confirmation from an outside source. On the recommendation of a friend, a prophet of God is brought in.

His name is Micaiah. Ahab soon learns that God has granted this little-known man snorkel vision: while living on earth, he can see directly into Heaven. He actually watches and listens as God responds in real time to Ahab's question.

Let's watch with him:

> *I saw the LORD sitting on His throne, and all the host of Heaven standing by, on His right hand and on His left. And the LORD said, "Who will persuade Ahab to go up, that he may fall at Ramoth Gilead?"*
> *So one spoke in this manner, and another spoke in that manner. Then a spirit came forward and stood before the LORD, and said, "I will persuade him." The LORD said to him, "In what way?"*[1]

Do you see what's happening in Heaven? It could almost be called a business meeting. God wants to rescue Israel from its evil king, but He's open to ideas on how to accomplish it.

When the spirit (or angel) proposes to mislead the king through his advisors, God not only approves but promises him success.[2]

On earth Micaiah warns Ahab that his advisors have been misled. But the king decides to listen to them anyway. He confidently marches north against Syria, only to die in battle.[3]

But wait, you might be thinking. *How does this historical incident help me know how to partner with Heaven to deliver a miracle?*

Let me show you. Since every miracle from God begins in the supernatural realm, we first need to find out how Heaven works. Which brings us back to Micaiah. His extraordinary glimpse behind the veil of Heaven shows a clear connection between events in Heaven and simultaneous events on earth.

And it reveals two surprising insights about what God is doing right now that could completely change how you think about your miracle potential. They did for me.

Let's start with the first one.

God's to-do list

Could it be that God has work to do and that He is working right now on an agenda—a kind of daily to-do list?

The prophet sees that God is surrounded by "all the host of Heaven standing by, on His right hand and on His left." We know from elsewhere in Scripture that the hosts of Heaven are angels numbering in the millions. At least in this scene, not one of them is singing. It looks to me as though they've been summoned to a meeting with God. He wants to influence someone's day on earth, and believe it or not, He's open to ideas on how to accomplish it.

While most of us think God is still resting from the demands of Creation week, the Bible shows another picture. He has a real-time, right-now agenda on earth.

God with a to-do list? The implications are profound.

But Jesus showed that it's true. To those who criticized Him for healing a man on the Sabbath, Jesus said: "My Father is always at His work to this very day, and I, too, am working."⁴ Jesus clearly revealed that His work of healing on the Sabbath was a continuation of God's ongoing work on earth.

Then Jesus went on to describe an active partnership:

*The Son can do nothing of Himself, but what He sees the Father do; for whatever He does, the Son also does in like manner. For the Father loves the Son, and shows Him all things that He Himself does.*⁵

So all during Jesus' lifetime on earth, Father and Son were hard at work on Heaven's to-do list. God intervened in human affairs, and amazing miracles resulted!

Since Jesus is no longer on earth, we need to ask whom God is looking to now to complete His agenda. Micaiah's glimpse behind the veil can change how we think about that too.

Let's revisit the scene in more detail.

> *It sure sounds like God is looking for a volunteer. And He's obviously open to suggestions.*

Inside Mission Central

The prophet sees that God is holding a meeting. The hosts have been assembled for a strategy session. "Who will persuade Ahab to go up [to war]?" God wants to know. It sure sounds like He's looking for a volunteer. And He's obviously open to suggestions. As Micaiah watches, an angel comes forward to volunteer. He says he has a strategy in mind that will persuade Ahab.

"In what way?" God asks.

When the angel tells God his plans, God approves and sends him on his way. "You shall persuade him, and also prevail," He says. "Go out and do so."

Which brings us to the second surprise:

Could it be that Heaven today should be thought of as Mission Central, where God is actively looking for and sending out volunteers who will carry out His agenda on earth?

We know from Scripture that God has three options for getting something done on earth:

- *In Person,* as when He dictated the Ten Commandments to Moses
- *By an angel,* as when the angel Gabriel announced the upcoming birth of Jesus to Mary

But from Scripture and history, we must conclude that God has chosen these options only rarely. That leaves...

- *Through a human being*

Think about it: today, tomorrow, and the day after, our all-powerful God will choose to work through ordinary people to get done on earth what He has decided in Heaven that He wants to do.

If God is so intent on finding volunteers, it only makes sense that He would communicate His wishes to human beings everywhere. It only makes sense that Mission Central would be sending out requests—miracle missions included—to people all over the world all the time.

But that can't be true.

Or can it?

Signals sent, signals not received

When *The Prayer of Jabez* was still at the top of the *New York Times* bestseller list, I was invited to speak in Hollywood at an unusual gathering of movie-industry insiders. The film director who called said that his colleagues—most of them agnostics or atheists—couldn't figure out why a book on prayer was outselling Stephen King and John Grisham.

"I've been working in this business for twenty-six years, and this is the first time an evangelical Christian has been invited to speak," he said when he picked me up at my hotel. "I'm guessing the crowd will be small—maybe twenty or thirty."

But God was up to something. We walked into a packed house of at least four hundred. I had just started explaining the second part of the Jabez prayer—"Lord, expand my territory!"—when a man in the back interrupted.

"I have a question!" he shouted. "Do you really believe that prayer works?"

"Yes sir, I do."

"Every time?"

"Yes."

"Get out!" He clearly wasn't buying it.

"Let me ask all of you a question," I said. "How many of you would say that at least once in your life you were clearly nudged to stop and help a person but you didn't?"

Almost everyone in the room raised a hand. Instinctively they recognized that they had been nudged to act by a supernatural force.

"That's why God always answers the prayer of a person who wants to do more for Him," I told my audience. "Because God nudges everyone, and almost everyone says no!"

Are you beginning to see why you can be a part of as many miracles for God as you want? Everywhere around us God has urgent work to be done. At all times He is looking for volunteers who will partner with Him. And He isn't just passively on the lookout; He is actively, constantly, and passionately sending out requests.

You'll learn to be a living link between Heaven and earth, recognizing a miracle opportunity where others see nothing at all.

Later in this book I'll show you how miracle agents can develop new sensitivities—or rediscover buried ones—that will help them stay in tune with God's intentions. For example, in chapter 8 you'll find helpful teaching on miracle-specific signals from God, from others, and even from yourself. By learning to read the signs effectively, you'll learn to be a living link between Heaven and earth, recognizing a miracle opportunity right in front of you where others see nothing at all.

By now you might be wondering why anyone would miss Heaven-sent invitations to a miracle. In my experience longtime Christians are especially susceptible to missing them because of a common misunderstanding about God's motivations.

I suffered from it for years.

Praying (fervently) for the wrong thing

Early one morning I was asking again for God to do a miracle in the life of a friend. My part (I thought) was to persuade God to answer in a big way. Specifically, I was earnestly asking God to use me to deliver a miracle in my friend's life. What could I do or say that would change God's mind and release His favor? What kind of intensity or desperation would it take on my part to get God's attention?

Suddenly, in midprayer, I felt compelled not to say another word. I felt drawn instead to reflect silently on the assumptions hiding underneath my prayers. What did they tell me that I *really* believed about God and His desire to act? What did they reveal about how I thought God was hearing my prayers at that very moment?

It didn't take long for my actual theology of prayer to rise to the surface. Clearly, I believed that God was reluctant to do miracles. That's why I needed to try to persuade Him—give Him reason after reason, day after day, so He would finally relent and decide to act.

In the middle of these thoughts a familiar Bible verse came to mind:

The eyes of the LORD run to and fro throughout the whole earth, to show Himself strong on behalf of those whose heart is loyal to Him.[6]

Now, I'd always understood this verse to mean that God wants loyal servants. And of course He does. But for the first time I read these words for what they showed me about what God is doing in Heaven right now. Do you see it?

God is not reluctant or uninterested when it comes to showing Himself strong. Rather, He is looking "to and fro throughout the whole earth" for people who are loyal to Him. Why? So He can reveal His supernatural power in their lives!

Let me summarize what we've learned so far about partnering with Heaven for a miracle:

- God is constantly at work in supernatural ways in our world, and He has much He wants to get done.
- God is actively looking for loyal partners—people who consistently care about what He cares about.
- God is regularly nudging people to respond, but most people miss His intentions or simply say no.

What would it look like in your life if you started saying yes? Let me share a family story.

A network of nudges

When our daughter Jessica was a teenager, she went with a group on a short-term mission to Europe. Their purpose was to assist local churches in youth outreach, but along the way Jessica found that her most important ministry seemed to be with Leila, a girl her own age in the group. As the two girls became friends, Leila began to confide in Jessica. A family member was sexually molesting her, she said. Jessica was the first person she felt safe enough around to reveal what was going on.

Jessica listened in shock. "What's happening is not your fault," she told Leila. She made Leila promise to get help immediately.

Not long after Jessica returned to the States, our family moved to Africa. But Jessica and Leila stayed in touch by phone and e-mail. Even though Leila's circumstances didn't improve, she resisted getting help. Then she seemed to drop off the map.

One afternoon Jessica sensed strongly that Leila's situation had reached a crisis point. She couldn't explain the feeling—she and Leila had been out of touch for a month. But Jessica decided to act. She called and e-mailed a network of Christian friends, including some friends from the mission trip. Her urgent message read: "I don't know why, but I think something terrible is happening with my friend Leila. Please pray for her right now!" Jessica still had no idea whether Leila was okay or not, but she had decided to act on the leading she felt.

The next day a friend called with news. Two hours after her friends had started to pray, Leila had made a serious attempt to take her life. Thankfully, she hadn't succeeded.

"I'm so glad I acted on what I sensed God was telling me," says Jessica. "I believe Leila is alive today because of the desperate prayers of friends. Her narrow escape convinced her to break the silence and get the help she needed."

Today Leila is full of life and happily married.

What do you think could have happened if Jessica had decided not to follow that nudge from Heaven? My second story illustrates what can happen when people ignore what God wants.

The consequence on the corner

A few years ago our creative team was shooting a feature film in South Africa in the dead of winter. The story centered on a Zulu boy who became orphaned when his parents and relatives all died of HIV/AIDS. To survive, the boy left his village and took up a hardscrabble existence fending for himself on the streets of Johannesburg.

One bitterly cold winter morning our crew was scheduled to begin shooting at five o'clock on a particular street corner. It was so cold that production assistants had arrived early to set up tents with gas heaters where we could keep ourselves warm. We all showed up at the set wearing scarves, gloves, and heavy coats—not the attire that usually comes to mind when people think of Africa.

By the time I arrived that morning, several police cars were already there, emergency lights flashing. The film team looked as if they were in the depths of despair. I asked the director of photography what was going on.

"I can't believe this," he told me somberly. "Last night, right across the street, a homeless boy froze to death. They found him this morning."

I was stunned. Everybody was. Then, as we contemplated what had happened, the terrible irony set in.

Here we were to shoot a scene about a homeless orphan, and right across the street a homeless orphan boy died because no one gave him a blanket or a coat. No one gave him shelter.

Finally I said to the crew, "You don't think that boy's death reflects God's heart, do you?"

Based on what you've learned in this chapter, what do you think? Wouldn't you say that God heard the prayers of that little orphan boy, decided to intervene, and began nudging all kinds of people toward him? But no one came.

That would mean what God urgently wanted to happen on that winter morning in Johannesburg didn't happen. Someone—perhaps dozens of people in different places during the preceding days—said no to Heaven's nudge.

A door marked "Yes"

In the opening chapters of this book, we've seen that each of us was created for nothing less than a miracle-filled life. It's not a special existence reserved for the select few but is for everyone.

We've seen that a life marked by the miraculous is not just possible, not even just desirable, but is at the very center of God's will for every one of us. When we settle for less, our lives lose delight, fulfillment, and purpose. Personal needs of people we meet get overlooked. Extreme needs in our communities and around the world go unmet. When a whole generation settles for less, the character and motives of God get called into question. His shining presence seems to fade in the world.

But you were born to be a living link between Heaven and earth. You were born to be God's ambassador in the Everyday Miracle Territory, making Him visible in unforgettable ways.

When a whole generation settles for less, the character and motives of God get called into question. His shining presence seems to fade in the world.

The miraculous touches of Heaven that God wants to accomplish will come in all sizes, but mostly they'll be of the personal, everyday sort that you can be a part of. Why? Because God passionately desires to show Himself strong for you and through you, and because every person you meet has a significant need that only God can meet.

In the coming chapters I'll show you how to step into a lifestyle of miracles. You begin by picking up and putting to work four keys to a life of predictable miracles.

The first key is the simplest and the most profound. You'll find it at a door marked "Yes."

Part 2

FOUR KEYS TO A LIFE OF MIRACLES

Introduction to the Miracle Life Keys

All seven miracle keys I talk about in *You Were Born for This* describe specific actions that unlock the miraculous in our lives. Each key is based on powerful biblical insights about how Heaven works. And each leads to a breakthrough in our potential to partner supernaturally with God in His work on earth.

The seven keys fall into two groups. Special Delivery Keys (Keys 5–7) apply to specific needs. They are external actions we take that lead to a miracle breakthrough for another person. We'll look at these in part 4.

The Miracle Life Keys (Keys 1–4), which I talk about next, describe internal actions that prepare you for a life of miracles. Each Miracle Life Key can become a habit that will radically change how you see the world and how you partner with God in the supernatural realm. Without these keys we would stand in the middle of Everyday Miracle Territory totally unaware of how to tap into the supernatural as a way of life.

Here's a brief preview:

> **The Master Key** is an urgent prayer to be sent by God on a miracle mission. Your request alerts Heaven that you are more than just available; you're committed to respond whenever God nudges you. It's called the Master Key because your urgent plea opens the door to a life of miracles.

> **The People Key** readies you for the inevitable moment when Heaven's agenda collides with your own. When you apply this key, you put yourself and Heaven on notice that you have decided to make God's heart for people your own. Because you now share His passion for people, you'll be

prepared to deliver miracles to whomever He asks whenever He asks.

The Spirit Key prepares you to cooperate with God's Spirit, especially in regard to His supernatural power. The action of this key releases you from any false assumptions about your ability to do a miracle and aligns you with the supernatural power that's always required to accomplish a miracle outcome. As you learn more about how the Spirit works through you, you will come to rely on Him with increasing confidence.

The Risk Key shows you how to intentionally live in such a way that you take risks of faith, relying on God to accomplish what He wants done. You act in dependence on God despite feelings of discomfort or fear, trusting that He will bridge the gap between what you can do and what only He can do through you. When He bridges that gap with a miracle, His power and glory are on display.

These keys are practical, doable, and biblical. They position you to experience God's supernatural power on a regular basis. And obviously, they will enhance your relationship with God as well.

Which brings us to an important question. Why did I include these four keys and not others?

Naturally, spiritual disciplines like Bible study, regular fellowship, acts of service, and prayer—along with consecration and obedience—are indispensable to Christian growth. But I chose these four keys because they specifically unlock, or make possible, a person's potential to partner with Heaven to do God's work on earth. The priority I have given them is based on the teaching of Scripture, considerable research, and my own ministry experience.

I'm not suggesting these are the only possible actions that influence our miracle potential. Other people could come up with valuable alternatives or additions. But these keys have proved essential and profoundly meaningful to me and many others over the years, and I'm confident they will prove the same for you.

You might particularly notice that I don't list prayer as a key. Prayer certainly plays an important part in miracle delivery, as you'll see numerous times in this book. But I chose not to make it a key for several reasons. First, because so much has already been written on this subject (including my own works *The Prayer of Jabez* and *Secrets of the Vine*). Second, because many use prayer indirectly to *avoid* taking action. For example, when we say, "I'll keep you in prayer," we often mean we don't intend to respond further. And third, the all-important focus of *You Were Born for This* is on what happens when God answers someone else's prayer by sending *us* to deliver a miracle.

None of the Miracle Life Keys alone is a guarantee that you will experience the miraculous. But the fewer of these keys you activate, the less likely you'll be to experience miracles. And conversely, the more you apply these powerful keys to align yourself with the way Heaven works, the more you will not only recognize miracle opportunities but also ask God to send you.

Taken together, these first four keys unlock a life of miracles. And by the time you combine these principles with the practical advice of parts 3 and 4 of this book, you'll have everything you need to begin delivering personal miracles.

4

The Master Key

You were born to be sent on miracle missions

O n a *steaming-hot* Georgia night, as I was driving home from visiting my mother, I made a request to God. It's one I've made many times in my life. Right there in my car, I pictured myself walking into the courts of Heaven, kneeling before the throne of God, and asking, "Please, Lord, send me to do Your work. I want to serve You this evening."

Minutes later I came to my next freeway exchange and took the off-ramp. That's when I noticed the older-model van up ahead, pulled off to the side. A man wearing a turban stood beside it, motioning for help.

I slowed down and pulled up behind him. By the time I had stopped, he was already at my window. "What's the problem, sir?" I asked.

"My van is broken down. I called for a tow truck, but they'll only take cash at night. I don't have any. I've been here for hours." He was soaking in perspiration and visibly traumatized.

"Come on around and have a seat in my car," I said. "It's cooler in here."

He got in, I handed him a bottle of water, and we talked about what to do. "You've really been out here for hours?" I said.

"Yes. And I've got small children waiting for me at home." He paused. "But what people have been shouting at me—that is the worst."

"Shouting?"

"Yes, as they drive by. I have never heard such filth. Racial slurs. Profanities. Curses upon my mother. They throw things…"

I knew then that my stop was not a coincidence or just an act of charity. The defeated man beside me was God's answer to my prayer only minutes ago. God had sent me, and He was nudging me to act on His behalf.

"I'm sorry, sir," I said. "Hours of that would be extremely painful." I turned to make eye contact. "If you'll allow me, I want to apologize for every disrespectful thing those people said." He looked at me in disbelief. "Please forgive us," I said. "That's not who you are. And that's not who everybody out there is either."

I told him I wanted to pay for the tow truck. I reached for an envelope in the daily planner on the seat beside me. "Here's something for the tow truck and a little more to get your van fixed. It's money I've been carrying for someone else. I have reason to believe He would want you to have it."

At first he was speechless. Then he thanked me profusely and asked for my address so he could pay me back.

"Nope. No need for that at all," I said.

He got out and walked toward his van. Then he paused, turned, and came back to my window. "Sir," he asked solemnly, "are you an angel?"

"Well, I was sent to you, but I'm not an angel."

"It was God who sent you, wasn't it?"

"Yes," I said.

Driving home, I was shaking my head in amazement at how God works. I had asked for a miracle appointment and taken my exit only minutes later, and there it was.

Have you ever asked God with all your heart to be sent on a miracle mission?

By "ask" I don't mean tell Him you're willing. I don't mean mention to Him that someday He could send you if He's really in a bind. I mean specifically, passionately, urgently plead with God to send you—and send you today!

I have seen a direct link in my life between that little prayer and extraordinary outcomes. Sometimes the appointments are on a small scale, like that night on the freeway. But sometimes they're larger. I've been sent to speak with CEOs of corporations, to negotiate peace between warring tribes in Africa, to help restore a marriage right before it ended in divorce, even to meet with presidents of countries.

What all these experiences have in common is this: they were initiated by a specific request on my part, and they ended with a miracle. When I asked to be sent, God sent me on miracle missions.

That's what the first key to a life of miracles is all about.

The kind of "yes" God is looking for

Your urgent request to be sent on a miracle mission is exactly the kind of "yes!" God is looking for. I call this purposeful move on your part the Master Key because it unlocks the invisible door between you and the Everyday Miracle Territory. Your action opens it, you step through, and everything changes.

What was once just the terrain of your life has now become a landscape brimming with miracle opportunity. Turn this key, and you are now fully acting upon your new job description as Heaven's delivery agent. You are a sent one from God on a mission inside the Everyday Miracle Territory.

By contrast, every other key I'll show you unlocks your miracle potential once you're there.

The Master Key is an urgent prayer to be sent by God to do His work. You enter the throne room of Heaven on a regular basis and ask God, "Please, send me!"

If you know the Bible, you might be thinking, *But why should I ask to be sent? Didn't Jesus already tell me to go?*

You're right. He did. Before He returned to Heaven, He passed His mission on earth to His disciples with an explanation. He said, "As the Father has sent Me, I also send you." Then He made that into a command: "Go into all the world and preach the gospel to every creature."[1]

But there's a problem. Have you noticed? Millions of Christ's followers already know what Jesus said. Millions agree that, since Jesus commanded us to go, it must be important. And millions are willing and available to go.

But so few go.

When you and I ask to be sent by God, we are taking His urgent, heartfelt *command* and turning it into our urgent, heartfelt *request.* We are coming all the way over to God's point of view on what we were born to do. We are declaring to God:

> I hear Your command, but I realize that hearing and agreeing are not enough. Therefore, I am sincerely asking, God, please send *me* today on a miracle mission. And I'm letting You know in advance, when You send me, I *will* go!

When you pray this way, God knows that He can call on you, His highly motivated delivery person, at any time. Whether He reaches into your heart with a nudge or simply puts you at the scene of something He wants done (as He did with me that night on the freeway), He knows you have already committed to act on His behalf.

Why *wouldn't* He begin to send miracle opportunities your way?

I used to think only those who knew the details of their mission in advance (and liked them) would ask so urgently to be sent. Then I looked again at the well-known story of how the prophet Isaiah asked to be sent.

I invite you to listen in on a most revealing conversation.

Eavesdropping on your future

In the book of Isaiah we find another account from a man who saw behind the veil of Heaven. Like Micaiah before him, Isaiah was permitted to eavesdrop on a conversation around God's throne. But unlike Micaiah, Isaiah didn't just politely listen and learn. He joined right in.

You might be familiar with what he wrote about his amazing experience:

In the year that King Uzziah died, I saw the Lord sitting on a throne, high and lifted up, and the train of His robe filled the temple. Above it stood seraphim; each one had six wings: with two he covered his face, with two he covered his feet, and with two he flew. And one cried to another and said:

"Holy, holy, holy is the LORD of hosts; The whole earth is full of His glory!"

And the posts of the door were shaken by the voice of him who cried out, and the house was filled with smoke.[2]

What a scene! The courts of Heaven filled to bursting—filled with the Lord's robe, filled with smoke, filled with the cries of strange angel-beings, filled beyond all that with the wondrous presence of God. Just another day in Heaven. But on this particular day, a witness from earth has been invited to watch.

As you'll soon notice, what Isaiah sees in Heaven is strikingly similar to what Micaiah saw:

- He sees that God is at work, focused on Heaven's agenda for earth.
- He sees that God is looking for a volunteer to carry it out.

God is not sitting back while the centuries tick by, merely listening to angel choirs.

That's why in the previous chapter we described Heaven as Mission Central. God is not sitting back while the centuries tick by, merely listening to angel choirs. Instead He is focused on dispatching miracle missions to meet needs on earth. Sometimes He sends angels. But for face-to-face work in the physical realm, God looks for people who will say yes.

A few verses later Isaiah hears God asking two questions.

Also I heard the voice of the Lord, saying:

"Whom shall I send,
And who will go for Us?"

Then I said, "Here am I! Send me."[3]

Notice Isaiah's immediate response. The Hebrew he uses is in the imperative. Isaiah so intensely desires to be sent that he almost commands God to send him!

Send him to do what? Well, it turned out that Isaiah was going to speak for God in the courts of kings and deliver striking visions that still inspire readers today. But at that moment Isaiah didn't know what he had ahead of him. He didn't ask either. I think Isaiah was so captivated by what he was seeing that he forgot he was still in Jerusalem. And instead of holding back, he cries out, "God, send me!"

Why can you and I be so bold with God? One reason: we're asking God to accomplish through us what He's already made clear He urgently *wants* and *will* accomplish. What father wouldn't entrust the tasks that are dearest to his heart to a son or daughter who demonstrates that kind of loyal commitment?

Look again at the two questions God asks that day as Isaiah listens: "Whom shall I send?" and "Who will go for Us?" He's not asking the same question twice; both questions are important. For example, not all who are sent will choose to go. (Wait till you meet Jonah in the next chapter.) God is looking for volunteers who have committed without preconditions to go when He asks.

Isaiah's answer embodies the truth of the Master Key: *God is looking for men and women who want to do Heaven's work so much that they earnestly request to be sent. And when they ask, He will act.*

> *I've noticed something reassuring. When we ask to be sent by God, He matches each of us with people we can help.*

Match-ups for personal miracles

I've noticed something unexplainable and very reassuring. When we ask to be sent by God, He matches each of us with people we *can* help. He did so for me that hot night beside the freeway. He orchestrated an appointment for me with that stranded driver that was time, need, and resources specific. He'll do it for you too. Your chance of helping the people you meet is just as high as my chance of helping someone I meet. It's uncanny, and it's certainly not chance.

Recently on an airplane I had my Bible in front of me, and I asked God to send me to a person in need. A man on his way back from the rest room saw me reading and stopped to say, "Now, that's a good book." After we exchanged a few words, he took the empty seat next to me. When I asked what I could do for him, he said, "Just before I walked back here, I was reading the book of Proverbs and begging God to tell me what to do. I need two miracles today. My construction company is in big trouble."

I couldn't believe it. He asked God specifically for two miracles! As it turned out, his problems were rooted in organizational and leadership issues that I have taught and consulted on for years. By the time we finished, God had answered his prayer. "Who would have thought God would answer my prayer so quickly," he said, "and as I was on the way back to my seat from the rest room!"

I share that incident to make a point: even when we're sure we have little to offer, God matches us with situations and people uniquely and for a purpose. Mission Central is *not* a haphazard operation. God will match you with different people than He would me. Yes, we both said, "Please send me!" But He will send us on different missions. They'll both have God's fingerprints all over them, though. And we'll both know we were set up for a miracle by the King of the universe.

My Master Key U-turns

To activate the kind of remarkable partnership with Heaven I've described and to keep it flourishing as a lifestyle, most people need to redraw their assumptions about how Heaven works.

The A statements below represent what most people believe—and what you may have believed until now. The B statements realign your beliefs with biblical truth so God can release miracles in your life.

> **What I believe about being proactive**
> *Belief A.* God just wants me to be available and willing for Him to work through me in miraculous ways.
> *Belief B.* God wants me to ask proactively to be sent on miracle missions.

What I believe about who is responsible for
God's miracle agenda for me on earth

Belief A. God's miracle agenda for me is completely His responsibility, especially when it comes to something only He can do. I don't have any responsibilities regarding miracles.

Belief B. God's miracle agenda for me is primarily my responsibility to fulfill by the power of the Spirit. I was born to partner with Heaven on miracle missions.

Where do you see yourself in these belief statements? Are you ready now to put down old misconceptions and grab hold of new, miracle-releasing ones? There's simply no way to step into a life of miracles while you're still shackled by false beliefs. And you don't have to be.

Say the new truths—the B beliefs—aloud to yourself right now, write them down in your journal, and watch what God does next in your life.

Unfortunately, for too many of us, the idea of being sent to do God's work can sound high-minded, superspiritual, and out of reach. That's why I like to put it in everyday terms.

Profile of a delivery agent

Picture this:

A parcel deliveryman comes to your door. He's holding a box. Your name is on it. Something inside the box is for you.

Or picture this:

A parcel deliverywoman comes to your place of business. She's holding a stack of oversize padded envelopes. Your name is on all of them. What's inside each one is for you.

What do you see in these two familiar scenes? A man and a woman on a mission. Each has been sent to you with a delivery. Each brings a particular package to a particular address and a particular person. They know you're most interested, not in them, but in the package. They're just delivery people.

Now picture this:

You are that delivery person. You are sent from Mission Central. Your job each day—maybe numerous times each day—is to deliver a package from God to someone else. What's in the package? You don't know exactly, but you believe that since it's from God, it is good—very good.

When you and I purposely ask God to send us to do His work on earth, we take on a completely different role in our day. We are now people sent from God, His delivery agents. We walk out the door knowing that He could have a miracle (a delivery through us) for anyone we meet. Why? Because, from God's point of view, everyone, everywhere, at all times is in need. God knows about every need, and He cares about each one. That's why He loves to send servants who are passionate about delivering visible proofs of His goodness and glory.

The life I'm describing is one that even longtime Christians rarely dare to imagine for themselves. But you and I were born to do more than imagine it—we were born to live it every day.

You might think that you must somehow make yourself more worthy before He would favor you with a miracle mission. But as surprising as it may seem, the opposite is the case. As you'll see in chapter 10, you are the one doing the "favor." It only makes sense that in a world of nearly infinite need, where most people say no to miracle missions, Heaven could have a backlog of divine missions just waiting to be delivered.

It only makes sense that when you and I enter into His presence and request with all our hearts, "Please, Lord, send me!" He will act.

Imagine, then, how God might respond if we asked to be sent, not just once, but on a regular basis.

How to ask to be sent

Each of the keys discussed in this book reveals an action that needs to become a life habit if you want to be productive for God in the Everyday Miracle Territory. But it all starts with the Master Key.

Here are simple steps you can take on a regular basis so that your yes to God becomes a way of life, not just a one-time event.

1. *Consciously enter the throne room of Heaven.* In your mind picture walking into the magnificent throne room where God the Father sits with Jesus Christ at His right hand. Consider this as an actual event that takes place in the courts of Heaven rather than just words you pray. Following the example of Isaiah, come with your urgent request in mind.

2. *Volunteer with the words "Here am I. Send me!"* Picture yourself asking God with all your heart to choose you for His service. "Here I am. Please send me on a miracle mission!" That's all you need to say. That's all He needs to hear. That's how Isaiah addressed God when he saw the way Heaven worked. The Bible uniquely honors the "*fervent* prayer of a righteous man."[4]

3. *Precommit to act when you are nudged.* Pledge to God, "As You lead, I *will* respond." Sometimes you'll say those words to the Lord, while at other times you'll simply reaffirm that commitment to yourself. But the point is, no matter how, where, or when God signals His will, you have decided in advance to act. In fact, you have decided in advance that the greater risk is not misreading His nudge but getting sidetracked by rationalizations, excuses, uncertainty, doubt, or neglect.

4. *Actively put your faith in God to deliver His miracle through you.* Why? Because you'll be fighting fear before long. So exercise your faith by committing to God, "I trust You to deliver the miracle through me. Thank You that I can fully depend upon You!" Then you are done. Leave the throne room joyfully as a sent one.

Post it on your mirror, stick it on your dashboard or desk, or write it in your daily planner: "Today I am a delivery person for God. Please, Lord, send *me!*" The prayer is your signal to Heaven that you are on the alert and eager to serve.

Since you're now wearing the uniform of Mission Central, you can proceed on God's authority, confident about what lies ahead.

What comes next?

Of course, it's only natural to wonder what happens next. You'll soon see that leaving the unknowns to God becomes part of the adventure. But if you're like most people, you immediately suspect that you left Mission Central without something—something very important.

Directions, maybe?

A name?

A few hints?

I have good news. First, you can expect miracles to begin happening in your life right away, even if you don't learn any more specifics about your mission. It's true! I've seen it happen many times. God just loves to work with a delivery person who is bold enough to say to Him, "Send me, Lord, whatever that means and however it happens. I trust You."

Second, you're now ready to discover God's agenda for your day and to share His heart for the beneficiaries of your mission like never before.

That's what the next chapter is about.

5

The People Key

You were born to share God's heart for people

*S*ome years ago, while boarding a flight to Los Angeles, I had nothing in mind but meeting a deadline. My book *Beyond Jabez* was
about to go to the printer. This would be my last chance to make changes.

As I took my seat, I asked God to help me finish my work before we
landed in California. (But honestly, my prayer meant "Please don't ask me
to help anyone for the next three hours!")

Fortunately, I'd been able to upgrade to business class with frequent-flier
miles, and I figured the extra room would improve my chances of working
without distractions. And I had been seated next to a window beside an
empty seat—even better. I breathed a sigh of relief and thanked God for
hearing my prayer.

But just before the doors closed, I heard the voice of a loud and obviously
drunk man entering the plane. My heart sank. He couldn't be headed to the
seat next to mine, could he? Quickly I reminded God that the book I was
working on was His book. *Surely You want me to get this done!*

Then the man came into sight, swaying down the aisle. His hair was dyed several colors, and his body had been pierced in numerous interesting places. When he paused at my row, the smell of alcohol seemed to fill the cabin.

"Hey, I think this seat is mine!" he announced.

"Yes sir," I said. "I wondered if it would be."

Once seated, Rainbow Metal Man accepted a drink from the flight attendant. Then he wanted to talk with me. We traded chitchat for a few minutes, then I made my move—a not-too-subtle turning of my attention back to my work.

He made his move too. He ordered another drink.

I happened to be proofreading a section of the book that included stories about our family's time in Africa. I worked, and Rainbow Metal Man kept drinking until the attendant suggested he'd had enough. The whole time, I kept my body turned away from my companion as much as possible. Meanwhile, I kept defending my choices. *Lord, You know I can't talk to this guy. Don't let him interrupt me. I need to get these pages proofed!*

But after proofing so many pages about how Jabez asked to do more for God, I gave in. *All right, Lord,* I prayed. *Send me to serve You, even to this man. But let him start the conversation.*

I had no more prayed those words when Metal Man spoke up. "That's a @#!!@# good book!" he yelled.

"Uh, you think so?" I said. I didn't know quite what to say. It was the first time a person had ever sworn about one of my books (at least in my presence). "How do you know that?"

"@#!!@#! I've been reading it over your shoulder!"

I nodded, trying not to get tipsy from the fumes.

"But I have an important question," he announced. "Are you a priest?"

Where on earth did that come from? I wondered. I wasn't wearing black clothing, a clerical collar, or a cross. I was about to say no when a verse flashed into my mind:

You are…a royal priesthood, a holy nation, His own special people, that you may proclaim the praises of Him who called you out of darkness into His marvelous light.[1]

"Yes," I stammered. "I guess you could say that I'm a priest. But what makes you ask?" I turned to him. "By the way, I'm Bruce."

Rainbow Metal Man was actually named Gary. He settled back in his seat, took a deep breath, and then told me exactly why God had sat him next to me. Of course, he didn't use those words, but that's what came through loud and clear to me.

"I'm flying out to Hollywood 'cuz I'm in charge of a sold-out rock concert at the Rose Bowl," he said. "But my best friend in the world was in an accident yesterday. He was killed."

"I'm so sorry," I said.

Gary sat in silence for a moment. "You know, when I went over and saw him dead, I couldn't help thinking, *If that was me, I don't know where I'd go after I die.*" He looked at me with bleary eyes. "I couldn't sleep all night. On the way to the airport, I said to God, 'If You are there, God, *please* send me a priest!'"

I laid aside my work then and picked up my miracle assignment. "How can I help you, Gary?" I asked.

Anyone, anytime, anywhere

Do you believe that God can reach through a haze of alcohol if He wants to deliver a miracle? I do now. I'm so grateful God interrupted what I thought was important that day on my flight to L.A. If He hadn't, I would have missed Gary—the miracle appointment God had lovingly guided to the seat next to mine.

What would have happened if I had said no?

In the previous chapter we saw how the Master Key starts you in motion as God's delivery agent. If you've prayed to be sent, you're now ready to work for God in the Everyday Miracle Territory. But as my Gary story illustrates, being sent is just the beginning. What comes next takes nearly every delivery agent by surprise. I call them *collision moments,* and you will encounter them over and over in your life.

Here's how they happen.

You and I set out with the best of intentions to serve God. But we bring with us expectations and assumptions about what our new miracle life will look like—how God is going to work through us, when miracles will happen, what kind of people we'll serve, and how they will respond to us once the miracle has been delivered.

I'm often forced to choose—not between something bad and something good but between something good and something miraculous.

There's a problem with all that, though. In my experience, God's miracle agenda for me rarely matches my expectations and assumptions. And when the miracle appointment arrives, I'm often forced to choose—not between something bad and something good but between something good and something miraculous.

If I'm not careful, I can miss my miracle appointment altogether.

Did you notice in my encounter with Gary how easily I mistook my agenda for God's? My plans sounded perfectly logical, even spiritual. I was working against a deadline on a book that could influence thousands of readers for God. Add it up: thousands of readers versus one inebriated, foul-mouthed Metal Man. No contest! I was 100 percent positive that I already knew Heaven's agenda for my flight, and it was spread out in front of me in black and white.

But I was wrong. Heaven's agenda for me was Gary.

Every miracle starts with a person in need. As obvious as it might sound, that fact is what makes this next key so critical.

The People Key is how you make God's agenda and heart for people your own. You prepare for the inevitable collision between your preferences and God's by yielding your rights in advance. That way He can deliver a miracle through you to anyone at any time.

I call it the People Key because God's entire agenda with regard to miracles can be summed up in a single word: *people.* This key unlocks several important understandings of God's purposes for sent ones:

- Our personal agenda must surrender to His.
- Our heart in any miracle must be His heart.
- Our role in any miracle must be to serve people—anyone, anytime, anywhere He directs.

Serving people according to Heaven's agenda was certainly Jesus' top priority. "I am among you as the One who serves," He told His disciples. On other occasions He said, "The Son of Man did not come to be served, but to serve, and to give His life a ransom for many," and, "I have come down from Heaven, not to do My own will, but the will of Him who sent Me."[2]

Jesus was sent by Heaven to serve—and you and I are too.

If we aren't passionately and deliberately focused on carrying out God's agenda with God's heart, we'll end up putting our own agenda first. We'll increasingly look for the kind of mission we enjoy most. We'll tend to ask God to bless our busyness for Him instead of asking Him to send us on the miracle mission of His choice.

The People Key releases us to be more available for miracle deliveries because we've already agreed with Him on some very important issues. For example, we have agreed in advance that the person, place, nature, and timing of a miracle are up to Him, not us. We have surrendered our perspective, our wisdom, our experience to one thing—His miracle agenda for us at any given moment. We have affirmed with God that His miracle opportunity, when it comes, will always be a person or persons in need. And we have said to Him that we understand that the person in need may not look to us like an opportunity at all.

Jesus knew exactly what an unexpected opportunity for a miracle might look like. For Him, as for us, the person in need of a miracle might look like

- an unpopular person (Zacchaeus),
- a social outcast (the Samaritan woman at the well),
- an unacceptable interruption (the lame man let down through a hole in the roof),
- a late-night visitor (Nicodemus),
- a desperate person clutching at us in a crowd (the woman suffering from a hemorrhage).

To put it another way, our delivery opportunity is likely to come at the time or in the manner we'd *least* prefer:

- during our kid's basketball game
- at the store when we're running late
- when every last bit of our energy is used up
- in the middle of important work we're doing for God
- when we finally settle in for a long-awaited Sunday afternoon nap

Which brings us to the action step in the second part of our People Key definition: knowing that God's miracle appointments for me will often collide with my plans and preferences, I precommit to yield my rights to Him whenever He asks and to serve those in need.

Does this really mean we should be ready to deliver a miracle to any person we might meet? Yes. If we go into our day wearing our Preferred People sunglasses, filtering out the sight of those we'd rather not have to deal with, we'll miss a significant percentage of Heaven's miracle opportunities. Or we'll notice but say, "No thanks."

If we go into our day wearing our Preferred People sunglasses, we'll miss a significant percentage of Heaven's miracle opportunities.

That's exactly what Jonah did.

Mission unacceptable

You probably know Jonah from Sunday school or a children's picture book. But Jonah's story illustrates a grown-up truth: even though people are the reason God does a personal miracle, one of the biggest challenges to delivering those miracles is…people.

They can be so demanding and difficult, so unworthy and ungrateful. And of course *we* can be all those things too. Problem is, God doesn't seem to factor any of this in when He sends us on a mission. He certainly didn't when He sent Jonah.

Jonah was a prophet in Israel, so we know he had already said yes to being sent. But then came his collision moment. God asked him to go to Nineveh, the capital city of Assyria, with an important message: if you don't repent of your evil ways, God will destroy you. Now, the Assyrians were a notoriously violent nation of idol worshipers and were age-old enemies of Israel. In Jonah's opinion their destruction, not their repentance, sounded like the perfect plan.

So when God asked, Jonah said no and ran in the opposite direction.

Here are scenes from the YouTube clip of what happened next:

A dusty road: Angry Jonah stomps his way to the coast. His every step shouts, *No! No! No!*

A busy port: Angry Jonah buys passage aboard a ship.

Storm at sea: Ship plunges through huge waves.

Stormier at sea: Ship takes on water. Desperate crew throws cargo overboard.

Stormier still at sea: Ship about to go down. Desperate crew throws Jonah overboard.

Calm day at sea: No sign of Jonah.

But three days later there's an incredible turn of events—a big fish deposits Jonah, slimy but alive, onto dry land. What a shock! Instead of delivering a miracle *through* Jonah, God has done a miracle *for* Jonah—and it's a whopper.

Now is he ready to serve? God wastes no time in finding out:

> *The word of the LORD came to Jonah the second time, saying, "Arise, go to Nineveh, that great city, and preach to it the message that I tell you." So Jonah arose and went to Nineveh, according to the word of the LORD.*[3]

This time Jonah obeys, and when he delivers God's message in Nineveh, Jonah witnesses his second whopper miracle—all 120,000 people in the city repent. God responds to their repentance by sparing them from destruction. Miracle mission accomplished for everyone.

Everyone, that is, except Jonah.

You'd think that two astonishing miracles in a row would have revamped Jonah's understanding about his role as a miracle delivery person. You'd think he would now be thrilled, convinced, and highly motivated to continue serving whenever and whomever God asks him to. But Jonah is not thrilled. The Bible says, "It displeased Jonah exceedingly, and he became angry."[4]

In fact, right through to the end of the chapter, Jonah argues with God about His plans and His motives. He's sure God has made a big mistake. Bottom line: *Jonah cannot accept that God's mission for him is to show God's compassion to people he doesn't like.*

It's easy to read the book of Jonah as an entertaining story of a stubborn prophet who would rather drown than let the wrong people know God loves them. But do you also feel the sadness in Jonah's story? He *knew* he was born to serve God. He *knew* he had been sent. And he *knew* beyond a doubt that God had showed up in his life with mercy and miracles. But it all seems wasted on him. I'd have to say Jonah failed the people test. Why? Because he refused to love others the way God loved him.

The apostle Paul wrote:

God demonstrates His own love toward us, in that while we were still sinners, Christ died for us.[5]

This is God's heart—while we were still unworthy and ungrateful, Christ died in our place. And this is God's heart too—if you're on the run from your miracle mission, God will patiently pursue you, right up to your last self-absorbed complaint.

The miracle power of the People Key lies in your choice to make God's self-sacrificing passion for people your own.

Whom do you serve—really?

It's time to ask the important question: what does it take to bring God's heart for people into every miracle opportunity—not just for a while, but as a way of life?

If we're in this to serve only those we want to serve, we'll eventually wear out. Like Jonah, we'll start looking the other way when God nudges us toward a miracle appointment. We'll be tempted to call in sick, to say to God, "Could You send someone else today?"

I remember the day more than twenty-five years ago when I confessed to a mature friend that I was losing my heart for ministry. "It's just too hard," I told him. "Half the people don't like what I'm doing, and the other half don't even know I exist!"

"Well, why do you do it?" my friend asked.

"What do you mean, 'Why do I do it?' God tells us to serve one another!"

"Yes," he replied, "but is that all He tells us about serving people?"

I didn't understand what he was getting at.

He continued. "Bruce, if you're determined to serve people for the sake of people, you'll eventually burn out and quit. And you'll quit for a very good reason."

"What is that?" I asked.

"Serving people just isn't worth it."

I was shocked. I had no idea that such a mature and highly respected Christian leader could feel that way. But he wasn't finished.

"Look, you have been called to serve God—and that's always worth it. But one of the ways you serve Him is by serving others. You have to keep your eyes on Him, because otherwise you won't last. Once you're focused on serving and pleasing God, the rest becomes irrelevant."

Then my friend reminded me of an important verse for servants:

Whatever you do, do it heartily, as to the Lord and not to men...for you serve the Lord Christ.[6]

Remembering whom you serve lies at the heart of the People Key. See in every face the face of Christ. Serve Him in "the least of these."[7] Put His heart and His agenda for people first. That's how sent ones stay in motion for a lifetime with the right motives and right priorities toward the right destination for God.

Heaven's right of way

If the People Key unlocks a sustainable life of delivering miracles, what keeps so many from picking it up?

I can identify at least three common wrong beliefs that stop well-intentioned sent ones from getting far in the miracle life they want. See where you find yourself in each set of statements:

Choosing the appointment God has for me

Belief A. If I'm busy doing good things, I'll be less likely to miss my miracle assignment.

Belief B. Since I can easily miss my miracle assignment even while I'm busy doing good things, I need to stay alert for God's direction.

Understanding the people problem

Belief A. I should serve others if they are worthy and grateful.

Belief B. I should serve others because I am serving God and showing His heart for people. Whether or not I feel they are deserving or grateful is irrelevant.

Sustaining a lifestyle of miracles

Belief A. Once I experience a miracle, my new way of life will sustain itself. I won't have to worry about personal motives and priorities getting in the way of God's plans.

Belief B. I can sustain a lifestyle of delivering miracles only by having God's heart for people, putting God's plans ahead of mine, and serving "as to the Lord."

I hope you have noticed a shift in what you believe. I hope you are adopting the B beliefs. You were born to serve others for God, in His way, with His heart.

You can make the People Key your own today with what I call a Declaration of Right of Way. Think of it this way: When you plead with God to send you to do His work by His power, your delivery van leaves Mission Central. You carry with you miracles known only to God for people identified only by Him. But now you know that between your front door and your delivery destination you're likely to encounter a collision moment—that point where God's agenda for you and your agenda for you will run into each other.

Decide in advance to surrender your rights to choose your own miracles, make your own plans, and serve your own Preferred People.

How can you prepare in advance to avoid these smash-ups? That's what the People Key is all about. You decide in advance to surrender your rights to choose your own miracles, make your own plans, and serve your own Preferred People.

You can do that by turning your new convictions into a personal agreement to yield your preferences to God before a collision even happens.

Declaration of Right of Way

Since I know that my own plans and preferences will often be on a collision course with God's miracle agenda for me, I surrender my rights in advance to God.

- I willingly take up my role as a servant, following the example of Christ.
- I view every person I meet as a potential miracle opportunity, no matter how surprised or unprepared I feel.

- I agree in advance to yield to God the details of time and place for my next miracle appointment.
- I surrender my expectations, rights, and preferences.
- I put down my expectation that those I serve should be worthy or grateful, because I serve everyone "as to the Lord."
- I place my busyness for God and any other good work in second position to God's leading in the course of a miracle delivery.
- I commit to seeing others through His eyes and responding to them with His heart, not mine, asking the Spirit to help me.
- I take off my Preferred People glasses and choose instead to view those I serve—including those I find most challenging or unappealing—as Christ Himself, because "inasmuch as you did it to one of the least of these My brethren, you did it to Me."[8]

Therefore, I no longer own the rights to how I serve. Those belong to God.

_____

Name and date

Where won't He send us next?

From God's perspective, the real miracle on my flight to Los Angeles was what God did in Gary's heart as we talked quietly about friends and death, Heaven and hell.

From God's perspective, the real miracle for Jonah never really happened. As far as we know, he never opened up his heart enough to let God's heart in. The four-chapter book of Jonah ends on a question mark. God asks Jonah, "Why shouldn't I care about your enemies too?"[9] We never hear Jonah's answer.

The promise of the People Key is that you and I get to write chapter 5 for our own "book of Jonah." By our action of exchanging our passions and priorities for God's, we place ourselves at the very center of what He cares about most. And what He cares about most is people.

Once we love people with God's heart, we line up our agenda with God's agenda. Imagine, then, how motivated God is to partner with us as often as possible to deliver as many miracles as possible to as many people as possible. Where won't He send us next? We have precommitted to accepting our next miracle assignment—whatever it is.

Now you're ready to cooperate with God's Spirit to accomplish what only He can—the miracle itself. That's what the next chapter is about.

6

The Spirit Key

You were born to partner with God's Spirit

illy Graham is coming to Caroni!" At least that's how we publicized the Friday night event around the village. Darlene and I were on the Caribbean island of Trinidad for a summer of ministry, and the small local church—built on stilts to catch the ocean breezes—had come up with a big plan: we had borrowed a projector and rented a Billy Graham feature for a free film night.

Each night leading up to the showing, church members gathered to pray that many would come. And each night one of the newest converts, a teenager named Radha, told us he knew his father would never come. "Jesus is not strong enough to bring my father," he said. We all knew that his father was the village drunk and despised followers of Jesus.

Friday night arrived. People kept filing up the stairs to the church. By the time we kicked off with songs and stories, we had a nearly full house.

Then we heard him—Radha's father standing in the street below swearing loudly at the church, everyone in it, and anyone named Billy Graham. There was nothing to do but proceed.

A fourteen-year-old girl stood to pray. She begged God to help Radha's father get through the door. No sooner had she finished than we heard someone climbing noisily up the stairs. Radha's father stepped in, scowled at everyone, and took a seat in the back row.

I smiled at Radha, then introduced the film. But when I flipped the switch, the unthinkable happened.

Nothing. Only minutes before, the projector had been working perfectly.

I began sweating profusely and praying for God to help. Several of us tried but failed to make the projector work. Then, as we fiddled with the machine, Radha's father stood, swore a blue streak, and stomped into the night. Soon after, his distraught son left too.

What should I do—keep working on the projector or deal with Radha? The Spirit's nudge was clear. *Go see Radha.* Leaving the projector to another person, I went outside.

I found Radha underneath the church, leaning against a stilt. He was sobbing. "I knew it!" he shouted at me. "I knew my father would never find out the truth about Jesus. Now he's gone forever!"

Despite the turmoil I felt, I sensed the Spirit leading me to take a bold step. "Radha," I said, "God was powerful enough to bring your father to the church the first time. He is powerful enough to bring him back. We are going to pray right now and ask the God of the universe to bring your father back, not only to watch the movie, but to meet Jesus tonight."

My throat tight with emotion, I prayed a simple prayer of faith for Radha's father. Then the two of us walked back into the church.

But one look at Darlene's eyes told me we were still in trouble. The projector had been given up for dead. People were getting ready to leave.

If ever we needed a miracle from God, it was now. Walking to the front,

I apologized for the disappointment. Then I felt nudged to pray one more time. "God, it's Your turn," I prayed. "We can't fix the projector, but You can!"

Then, feeling foolish and afraid, I reached for the On switch. Suddenly the projector whirred to life! Everyone raised a shout. God had demonstrated His power in a way we would never forget.

And He wasn't done. A few minutes into the movie, we heard footsteps on the stairs. It was Radha's father. Without a word he walked in and took his seat again.

When the movie ended an hour later, I gave an invitation. "If you want to put your faith in Jesus Christ like Billy Graham has explained, then would you please stand and come forward?"

The first to stand was Radha's father. With tears streaming down his face, he walked into the outstretched arms of his son.

That night a roomful of witnesses watched as the wind of the Spirit moved in our midst. We watched as He contended mightily with unseen powers and worked in the heart of an angry man to bring him to new life in Christ. And we watched as He showed His love and power to a doubting young man named Radha.

Ministry without the Spirit of God is merely our best efforts. Ministry with the Spirit of God is the stuff of miracles.

Ministry without the Spirit of God is merely our best efforts. Ministry with the Spirit of God is the stuff of miracles.

"Without You, I can't..."

With our next key, the process of unlocking a lifestyle of miracles will become more apparent.

First, the Master Key. You ask God to send you on a miracle mission.

Next, the People Key. You ask for God's heart for His agenda—people in need.

But now that you have been sent and share God's agenda, you will come face to face for the first time with a daunting question: how, exactly, are you supposed to deliver a supernatural event when you are so completely human?

That brings us to the Spirit Key. When you put this key to work in your life, you are formally aligning yourself with your heavenly partner—the Holy Spirit—to do God's supernatural work through you every day. You are telling God, "Without You, I can't do what You have sent me to do."

With the Spirit Key, you partner with the Holy Spirit to deliver a miracle by God's supernatural power. You precommit to cooperating with the Spirit at every opportunity to accomplish God's work.

The fundamental fact of the Spirit Key is that while you and I can *deliver* a miracle, only God can *do* a miracle. In fact, it's impossible to accomplish anything in the Everyday Miracle Territory without Him. And God works through us by His Holy Spirit.

But—have you noticed?—no other Person of the Trinity raises more confusion and disagreement among churchgoers. Some think of the Spirit as a benign but impersonal force, like gravity. Others count on Him for intense emotional experiences. In recent years much of the teaching on the Spirit has focused on His work inside us—His comforting presence, for example, or His role in making us more like Christ.

This chapter focuses purposely and exclusively on something else: the vital part the Spirit plays in our work as God's miracle delivery agents. We want to know, how does the Holy Spirit go about God's work in us and in the person we're talking to? And how do we cooperate?

If you have spent most of your life hard at work for God in the Land of Good Deeds, all this talk of partnering with an unseen person may seem like mere speculation. But it's not. The Spirit of God is a real and knowable Person in our world. And you and I were born to partner with Him for a life of miracles.

The Helper sent from Heaven

I often ask this question of people I meet: "What would you rather have: Jesus living as your next-door neighbor or the Holy Spirit dwelling in you as He already is?"

Did you hesitate? Many do, perhaps because it feels as if it requires them to choose between God and...God!

Others just go with their gut. "Well, Jesus, of course!" Why wouldn't a physically present God the Son be far better than an invisible God the Spirit?

It might shock you to know that Jesus already answered that question for us. We read about it in His conversation with the disciples the night before He was arrested. He reassured His friends that, although He would soon be leaving, He would send a Helper, the Spirit of Truth. Notice the reason Jesus gives:

It is to your advantage that I go away; for if I do not go away, the Helper will not come to you; but if I depart, I will send Him to you.[1]

Disciples' question: "Jesus, You're saying we're better off if You leave us?" Jesus' answer: "Yes, it is to your advantage."

Then Jesus explained the roles the Helper would have in the world. He would bring comfort, He would guide the disciples into all truth, and He would glorify Jesus.[2] Everywhere present in the world, God's Spirit would be released to do the work of Heaven. In all times and places, He would communicate with people's hearts, convicting them of their need of salvation, changing their destiny forever.[3]

It didn't take long after the coming of the Holy Spirit for the disciples to experience the astonishing advantage of the Spirit as their divine Partner. One day Peter said to a lame man, "In the name of Jesus Christ of Nazareth, rise up and walk." When the man jumped to his feet, an astonished crowd came running. But Peter was ready with an explanation:

Men of Israel, why do you marvel at this? Or why look so intently at us, as though by our own power or godliness we had made this man walk?[4]

"Don't misunderstand what just happened," Peter was in effect saying. "I'm not superpowerful. And I'm not superholy. In fact, I didn't and couldn't heal this man. God did it through me by His power, not mine."

What I want you to see is that today, centuries after Jesus' time on earth, we don't have less of God with the Holy Spirit. Whereas Jesus could be in only one place at a time, the Spirit is a gift to all believers all the time all over the world. Unlimited by a physical body, He dwells with us and in us at all times to testify of Christ. And only through His supernatural presence and power can we accomplish miracle missions.

What does partnering with the Spirit look like in someone's life? In the story about Radha and his father that opens this chapter, you saw just how inadequate I was in my own human power to accomplish what God wanted done. That meant I had to rely on the Spirit in many ways:

- to bring Radha's father to the event—and bring him back again
- to direct me to follow Radha outside rather than tend to the crowd and our technical difficulties
- to encourage me to pray boldly for Radha's father to return
- to nudge me to try to turn on the projector one last time
- to work in the father's heart to bring him to salvation
- to show Radha himself the power and goodness of our living God

But how can *you* partner with the Spirit?

A message for Marta

Lauren, a young woman I know, was away on a two-week assignment for her New York–based company. For the duration of the project, she stayed in the same hotel. Besides tending to her work commitments, Lauren found herself asking God to send her to do *His* work.

During her morning workouts in the hotel gym, she noticed a petite Hispanic woman who was always busily cleaning. When Lauren greeted her by name and asked how she was doing, the housekeeper always brightened. "Marta would look up at me, and her face would just beam," Lauren recalls.

Toward the end of her stay, Lauren stopped in at Target to pick up a few items. That's when Marta came to mind. God nudged Lauren to buy something for her to make her feel special. Unsure of what to do, but not wanting to miss out on what God might be doing, Lauren put together a small collection of feminine items, including lotion and scented bath salts.

Her last morning at the hotel, Lauren presented Marta with her gift. The housekeeper was surprised and delighted. "Thank you, thank you!" she said shyly. "You don't know how much this means. I am so tired at the end of the day. This is wonderful!"

Marta brought up the flowers that had been delivered to Lauren's room the previous day. "Oh, they are so beautiful!" she exclaimed. Lauren agreed that they were gorgeous.

Back in her room, Lauren was packing up to go when the Spirit nudged her again. This time it was about the flowers her husband had sent. *Those flowers are for Marta now. She needs to know that she is beautiful.*

Without hesitation Lauren went in search of Marta. "These are for you," she told her, holding out the flowers. "God wants you to have them."

Marta gasped. She grabbed Lauren's hand and pulled her into a nearby room. "You don't understand why this means so much to me," she said, her eyes filling with tears. "No one ever notices me. They don't even say hello. The past two weeks I've looked forward to coming to work because I know you see me. And now you show me that God sees me too."

I have little doubt that the housekeeper will always remember the day God sent her two extravagant reminders of His love.

Did you spot the Spirit at work in Lauren's story? Lauren asked to be sent. Then God led Lauren to give the housekeeper a gift. Lauren had no idea of Marta's need, but the Spirit knew it precisely. And through Lauren, He was able to speak directly into Marta's heart: "I see you, and I want to give you flowers today."

Lauren's story shows the kind of heart-specific miracle that God can deliver through any one of us when we are sensitive to the direction of His Spirit.

How the Spirit works

How do God's Spirit and God's servants work together, practically, to deliver a miracle? We focus on this in depth in the how-to chapters coming up on signals and steps. But for now, consider some ways the Spirit does what we cannot do during a miracle encounter:

The Spirit knows the other person. The Spirit, who "searches all things," has intimate, complete knowledge of everyone, including the people He sends us to help.[5] He knows what they were thinking when they woke up, what happened to them at work yesterday, and what secrets they plan to keep until they die. He knows what kind of gift or encouragement they're likely to refuse or deflect and what kind of gesture will go straight to their heart.

The Spirit knows us. The Spirit also knows our strengths and weaknesses, our fears and limitations, and leads us purposefully to a person in need. Not that God's Spirit is an impersonal force moving objects around on a chessboard. He is a Person. He knows everything about us, loves us perfectly, and can perfectly match us with the right person at the right time to deliver the right message.

The Spirit guides us. Jesus said, "When He, the Spirit of truth, has come, He will guide you into all truth."[6] How do we experience this guidance?

Lauren's story shows that responding to the guiding of the Spirit will usually be a natural process. To a person who is outside the process, being sensitive to the Spirit's leading may seem too mysterious to understand or trust. But during a God-arranged encounter—when you have asked to be sent and are passionate about partnering with God to accomplish His agenda—you will know what God wants. God's promise is this:

> *I will instruct you and teach you in the way you should go;*
> *I will guide you with My eye.*[7]

For most people, God guides us more than we realize. We don't have to look inside for a special emotion or inner voice. The Spirit will guide us *while we are in motion* to serve God. The New Testament uses words like "led," "compelled," and even on rare occasions "were forbidden" to describe how the Spirit communicates God's purposes to His servants.[8] Our part is to begin doing as much as we know He wants from us and then keep expecting further guidance.

The Spirit speaks of the Father and Son. Everything the Spirit does is directed by God the Father, and it's for one purpose: to accomplish Heaven's agenda and to bring glory to Jesus, God's

During a God-arranged encounter, you will know what God wants.

Son. When He works in the heart of the other person, He is communicating the truth to that person about his or her need, God's character, and the Person and work of Christ.[9] As you'll see in many instances in the chapters ahead, one of the most thrilling moments of a miracle delivery is when you look into the face of a person and realize, "God is here! He is at work. I am witnessing His work right before my eyes!"

The Spirit empowers us. Three times in Acts 4 the disciples are described as sharing the gospel with boldness. For example: "Now when [the religious leaders of Israel] saw the *boldness* of Peter and John, and perceived that they were uneducated and untrained men, they marveled. And they realized that they had been with Jesus."[10]

Remember, these were the same men who only weeks before had cowered in fear when Jesus was arrested. What changed? The Father had sent the Spirit, just as Jesus had promised, and they had experienced His power.[11]

You and I have that same Spirit working powerfully through us when we ask to be sent on a miracle mission. Yes, the task is too big for us. But we don't do it alone. We are in partnership with God's Spirit, and that makes all the difference.

The Spirit does the miracle. We are partnering with the most powerful force on earth—God Himself. And the Holy Spirit has been given to us so we can do good works by His power. He is our Helper. He is the only one who does a miracle. You and I are simply blessed to be invited into partnership with Him.

But we do the work! I like to say that although the Spirit carries the load, we should approach our partnership as "100 percent Spirit, 100 percent me." We are to do the work, and the Spirit empowers us to do it. So if you are guided to witness, to show compassion, to help the poor and needy, or to give of your resources, then your part is to open your mouth, your heart, your wallet—to get started. The Spirit will give you boldness, guidance, information, and everything else you need *in the process* of your obedience, not separate from it.

Given the power and promise of our divine partnership, what might be keeping you from taking up the Spirit Key and unlocking miracles in your life today?

New thoughts about the Spirit

It's time to look at our core beliefs about the Spirit's role in miracles. Nothing changes what we do like changing what we truly believe. Since beliefs determine behavior, misconceptions about the role of the Spirit as our essential partner in a divine mission keep millions from ever getting started.

See if you recognize your beliefs or unstated assumptions in these common misconceptions:

My understanding of the nature of the Spirit
Belief A. God's Spirit is too elusive, impersonal, and unpredictable for me to connect with in a practical way to deliver a miracle.
Belief B. The Holy Spirit is real, personal, and knowable, and I am invited to understand who He is and how He works, including in the area of everyday miracles.

My feelings and the Spirit's purpose
Belief A. The primary purpose of the Spirit is to help me feel spiritual or close to God, especially when I worship.
Belief B. The primary purpose of the Spirit is to help me accomplish God's agenda on earth.

My self-reliance versus partnership with the Spirit
Belief A. I can probably accomplish everything God wants me to do today by my own faithful efforts and discipline.
Belief B. I can accomplish everything God wants me to do today only by partnering with the Spirit.

My suitability to partner with the Spirit
Belief A. God will probably not have a miracle agenda for me today that would require my partnering with the Spirit, because I'm not specially trained or gifted.
Belief B. The Spirit is available equally to all who know Christ, and God may have a miracle agenda for me today that will require my partnering with the Spirit.

If you see yourself in any of the Belief A misunderstandings, you need to take ownership of your thoughts and change your mind. I can tell you from personal experience that wrong beliefs will absolutely keep you from using the Spirit Key to unlock a life of miracles. (For example, you won't be able to respond to the next key, the Risk Key, if you are following your own natural inclinations instead of walking in the Spirit.)

But when you change your thinking and start living by the truth, your miracle life will flourish.

Open letter to the Spirit

To take up the Spirit Key as transformative action in your life, first affirm your new, true beliefs from the previous section.

Then you may want to write the Spirit a letter of apology and commitment, as a friend of mine did.

Open Letter to the Spirit About Our Partnership

Dear Holy Spirit, I now recognize that every miracle is Your doing. Therefore, I apologize for how often in the past I have ignored or misunderstood Your guidance. I have often sidelined You and depersonalized Your role in my life. I have delegated the work You do to "professionals" and spiritual leaders. I have highly valued human solutions where only a supernatural act on Your part could bring Heaven's solution. I've done my best not to need You—not to live in partnership with You.

I'm sorry. How could I have been so foolish? Please forgive me. Now I know the truth, and I want to change.

I precommit to cooperating with You and following Your guidance every day, especially in every miracle opportunity You bring my way. I open my mind and heart to You, and I ask You to teach me in the days ahead how to partner with You in practical, joyful, and effective ways that bring Heaven to others and joy and honor to God. In Jesus' name I pray, amen.

[signed]_____

Becoming a skilled team player

Now that you have committed to partner with God's Spirit for miracles, you have signaled Heaven that God can count on you to do His work in His way to deliver a miracle.

Does this mean you should expect the Spirit to give you stunning visions as He did with His servant Isaiah and some other biblical figures? No. You're not them! God created you to be you. You can be confident that He will never set you up to fail. He will only ask that you take the next step He puts in front of you.

The exciting promise of the Spirit Key is that the more you purposefully partner with the Holy Spirit, the more He will release His power and intentions through you. When the Father has a miracle mission in mind, increasingly He will send you, one of His devoted team players.

When the Father has a miracle mission in mind, increasingly He will send you, one of His devoted team players.

In fact, prepare yourself to become one of God's favorite delivery people! Why? Because He knows you won't try to do the impossible alone. Instead, you will partner with His Spirit for miracle moments on earth.

7

The Risk Key

*You were born to take risks of faith
in dependence on God*

The traffic through downtown Atlanta went from slow to stop, and with it my hopes of catching my flight seemed to grind to a halt. What was I going to do? I was the only speaker scheduled for an important conference. As my departure time came and went, I prayed a desperate prayer you may have uttered as well: "Lord, please delay my flight!"

When I finally reached the terminal, well after the scheduled departure time, I ran up the escalator, feeling a little foolish even to be there. But blinking on the departures board was the word I'd hoped for: "Delayed."

At the gate I stared out the window and thanked God for what He had done. "Now I want to do something for You," I prayed. "Please send me a miracle appointment." I took a deep breath and turned around, believing, as I have so often, that the person God had in mind would become immediately apparent.

Standing next to me was a well-dressed businesswoman who had also just arrived at the gate. "It looks like you are glad the plane is late too," I offered.

She nodded.

I took a risk. "How can I help you?" I asked.

"What?"

"No, really, what can I do for you?"

"You can't do anything for me," she said matter-of-factly. Of course, why would she expect help to arrive in such an unusual way? But from previous experience I knew to give the Spirit time to work.

We chatted about other things, then I tried again. "I know my offer was unusual," I said, "but perhaps something's bothering you. Is there anything I can do?"

The woman seemed to calm herself, then to reach deep into her heart. "Actually, I'm flying home to divorce my husband," she said.

"I'm sorry to hear that," I said. "That must be why I'm here."

As we talked, her resistance began to melt. Her name was Sophie, and her professional manner and wardrobe couldn't hide her pain. Tears welled up in her eyes as she began to talk. Her husband had been unfaithful. Even though now he wanted to make things right, she had had enough. In her mind the marriage was dead. But as we talked, I was already reaching for a miracle key that you'll learn more about in part 4 of this book.

When our call came to board, we were the last to walk down the ramp. Sophie seemed concerned. "We aren't done talking about this yet," she said.

"Don't worry," I said. "We will sit together on the plane."

"What do you mean?" she said. "You don't even know what seat I have."

"I don't," I said. "But God does, and He'll put us together."

"God?" she exclaimed.

"If you were God," I said, trying to sound calm, "wouldn't you want us to sit together so we could finish this very important conversation?"

She shook her head in disbelief.

We compared boarding passes. We were five rows apart, and the flight was full. Now I was on the spot…and so was God.

Sophie took her seat, but as I got ready to take mine, the man in the seat next to her turned around and caught my eye. "I'll trade so you two can keep talking. I hate middle seats."

I'll never forget that flight. God showed Himself so strong and compassionate. By the time we landed, Sophie was a changed person. Even she could hardly believe what had happened. She had experienced a powerful miracle of forgiveness and had recommitted to giving her marriage another chance.

The indispensable step of risk

Now that you know the happy ending, I'll tell you that as I followed Sophie onto the plane, I wasn't brimming with confidence.

You see, I had taken a huge risk when I told Sophie, "God will get us seats together." I believed that God wanted us to continue our conversation. Still, I had no guarantee that He would act on the matter of seating. If He didn't, I'd look foolish, and any thought on Sophie's part that God was revealing Himself in her life might vanish.

You might be wondering, then, why I took such a risk. Couldn't God meet Sophie's needs in some other way?

My answer goes to the heart of this key. Twice I took an action that proved necessary to the miracle Sophie experienced. What were those actions? I purposefully *exercised my faith*—first when I asked how I could help her and again when I told her God would seat us together. I was asking God to reveal His goodness and compassion to Sophie in a miraculous way, and I proceeded in the faith that He would.

I took *risks* of faith.

You know what faith is—most people do.

"We believe!" we shout at ball games, meaning we can win this one if we just have faith. But this is faith in ourselves or in the team we're rooting for.

"Have faith in God," we say to each other, meaning we can entrust our lives and hopes to a good and powerful God. But this faith is usually passive, inwardly focused, and comforting. As important and wonderful as these faith expressions are, they are not the kinds of faith that I want to talk about in this chapter.

The faith I'm talking about here is directly related to how we partner with God for miracles. This faith is what we *do* because we believe God. That's why I describe it as active, outwardly focused, and usually very *dis*comforting. Knowing that we are sent and to whom we are sent, we take deliberate risks that place us in complete dependence on God for a miracle. By doing so, we declare to Him, "I believe You want to intervene in this situation, and therefore I will exercise my faith that You will. That way, when You act, Your goodness and glory will shine through."

Knowing that we are sent, we take deliberate risks that place us in complete dependence on God for a miracle.

When God came through that day on the plane, that's exactly what happened. Sitting in the seat next to me, surprise written all over her face, Sophie began to see that God had intervened in her day and that He deeply cared for her. We both knew that God would finish the miracle He had started. And He did.

In the previous chapter on the Spirit Key, you learned that God plays an indispensable part in every true miracle and that we must partner with His Spirit for a miracle to happen.

In this chapter you will discover *your* indispensable part. You must precommit to acting in faith, depending on God for a miracle. I call it the Risk Key.

The Risk Key is a purposeful action you take, in spite of discomfort or fear, to exercise your faith during a miracle delivery. Faced with an unbridgeable gap between what you can do and what God clearly wants

done, you take a risk to act anyway, depending on Him to come through. When God supernaturally bridges the gap, He enables you to deliver His miracle and demonstrates His glory.

How necessary is this key in the miracle realm? For example, if we don't take a risk of faith, will a miracle even happen?

These questions lead to an important observation. Perhaps you thought that God could do a miracle through you anytime He wants. But the truth is, He can't—or at least doesn't. How can I say that? Of course God is all-powerful. But Jesus Himself clearly stated that our faith has a direct impact on whether or not a miracle happens.

Sometimes, in fact, we prevent a miracle that God wants to do.

The connection between your faith and God's response

When Jesus' disciples asked Him why they couldn't do a particular miracle, He told them that they were limited because of their unbelief. Their unbelief, in other words, had literally stopped a miracle from occurring.

By contrast, He told them that if they had faith the size of a mustard seed, "You will say to this mountain, 'Move from here to there,' and it will move; and nothing will be impossible for you."[1]

What astonishing statements! Jesus' words reveal at least two important truths for sent ones about the role of faith in the miraculous:

- The amount of our faith is directly related to the likelihood that we will deliver a miracle.
- The amount of our faith is directly related to the size of the miracle we will deliver.

Notice also that Jesus doesn't say if you have a seed-sized faith in God, you *can* say to a mountain, "Move." His point is much more extraordinary. He says if you have a seed-sized faith, you *will* say to a mountain, "Move." Jesus is using the pictures of a seed and a mountain to help His listeners grasp the power of faith to exponentially impact the outcome. We might restate

His teaching like this: real faith in God so radically changes what you know is possible that it *will* change what you attempt *and* what you accomplish for Him.

Christ's amazing promise of faith should lead us to wonder, *What is hindering us from delivering great miracles? What other power pushes faith so far out of the picture that God does not even act?*

Jesus revealed the answer to that too. For example, we read that He didn't do miracles among people in His hometown of Nazareth "because of their unbelief."[2] Do you see the link? He wanted to do miracles; He encountered unbelief; He didn't do miracles. This cause-and-effect relationship shows how unbelief acts like a corresponding negative power to faith. Unbelief is the opposite of faith—and Jesus showed that it has the power to put a stop to miracles.

> *We must name our unbelief in our all-powerful God, wherever it lies, and reject it.*

Clearly, if you and I want to pursue a lifestyle where God works through us in supernatural ways whenever He chooses, we must take action. We must name our unbelief in our all-powerful God, wherever it lies, and reject it. Then we must *exercise* our faith. Why? Because there is a direct connection between what we initiate with faith and how God responds with His supernatural power.

One of my favorite pictures of the difference between unbelief and belief in action, between passive faith and risky faith, is the well-known story of Peter taking his unlikely step from a solid boat to…nothing but water.

Do you remember the scene? One blustery night the disciples were sailing across the Sea of Galilee through a storm. Suddenly a strange figure appeared, walking on the waves. The men were sure it was a ghost. But Jesus called out, "It is I; do not be afraid."[3]

In the next second (as far as we can tell), Peter got an idea. A very risky one at that. He said to Jesus:

"Lord, if it is You, command me to come to You on the water." So [Jesus] said, "Come." And when Peter had come down out of the boat, he walked on the water to go to Jesus.[4]

That first step—what an experience! What a risk! You can bet Peter remembered what that step felt like for the rest of his life. And all he needed to get him out of the boat and onto the waves was Jesus' command: "Come."

Interesting, isn't it, that everyone else in the boat stayed put? They had all spent the same months and years with Jesus, seen the same miracles, listened to the same teachings. They all held to the same correct theology.

But only Peter took a risk of faith—and only Peter experienced a miracle.

In spite of heart-pounding fear, Peter stepped out in proactive dependence upon God alone, believing that his faith would bridge the gap between the boat and Jesus. When Jesus did bridge that gap with a miracle, everyone in the boat "worshiped [Jesus], saying, 'Truly You are the Son of God.' "[5]

If you're familiar with the story, you know I'm leaving out everyone's favorite part. Out there on his watery stroll, Peter takes his eyes off Jesus, gets an attack of fright, and starts to sink. "Lord, save me!" he cries.

And immediately Jesus stretched out His hand and caught him, and said to him, "O you of little faith, why did you doubt?"[6]

It's easy to read those words and conclude that Jesus was chastising Peter. I don't think so. I think He was pleased with Peter's exuberant expression of trust.

The picture that comes to my mind is of a father, arms out, watching his baby daughter taking her first steps toward him. Can you imagine the moment? Baby's ready—eyes big as saucers fixed on Dad, a goofy smile pasted on her face. Then with a giggle she lets go of Mom's finger and starts toddling across the wide, wide world toward Dad.

Suddenly Baby realizes she has no idea what she's doing. She glances at the carpet. Her smile freezes. She falters, veers, and then *plop!* She's sitting on her bottom, wondering what just happened.

Now, what do Mom and Dad do at that moment? They applaud, of course. How do they feel? Proud as can be of Baby and her first step. It's a day they'll always remember. "You did great, sweetie!" they say. And in a minute, "Wanna try again? Now, look at Daddy this time. Just look at Daddy…"

Do you recognize a pattern? A risk of faith requires that we exercise our faith in such a way that we attempt what we cannot do, depending on God to do what only He can. But a one-time exercising of our faith is rarely all that's required. Not in my encounter at the airport. Not for a baby toddling across the carpet toward her dad. And not for Peter. Risks of faith are required *throughout* the miracle experience. Peter initiated a miracle with a big risk of faith. But later, when he focused on the waves instead of Christ, he let his fear overwhelm his faith. (I'll show you how to turn fear to an advantage when we get to the alert signal in chapter 8.)

But here's the bottom line: no matter what you and I believe, no matter what we feel, no matter how close we are to God, we don't have risky faith— and we won't experience miracles—so long as we're still in the boat.

The way to succeed in miracle delivery isn't to stay dry. It's to keep our eyes on what God wants to do, not on the watery depths or raging storms that stretch between us and the miracle. Then take that thrilling first step.

Change what you think about faith and miracles

For reasons we can only partly understand, God performs His greatest miracles when we act in complete dependence on Him. But let's be honest: almost everything about this kind of dependence goes against our instincts, our experience, and our common sense.

That's why, for most people, the Risk Key requires a significant change of thinking. Read these belief statements slowly and aloud to identify your old and new beliefs about the role of faith in your miracle life:

How my faith is linked to miracles

Belief A. Faith for miracles requires me only to believe in God, not to act upon that belief.

Belief B. Faith for miracles requires me to exercise my faith. Specifically, I must take proactive risks based upon what I believe about God and what I believe He wants done.

How risk unlocks a miracle opportunity

Belief A. In the course of a miracle mission, I should never put myself or God in a risky situation.

Belief B. During a miracle mission, my risk of faith is often necessary to unlock a miracle for another person.

How I should respond to discomfort or fear during a miracle opportunity

Belief A. When I feel discomfort or fear during a miracle mission, it is a sign that God must not be in it or that I am the wrong person for the job. Therefore, if I feel fear, I shouldn't proceed.

Belief B. I should proceed *in spite of* discomfort or fear. In fact, I should reinterpret those feelings as normal and even promising in the course of a miracle mission.

Each of the A beliefs describes a common assumption about how faith relates to miracle opportunities. And each one is an error and a trap. In fact, any one of them will significantly hinder your potential to partner with God's supernatural agenda in Everyday Miracle Territory.

By contrast, the B beliefs form the core truths of the Risk Key. Have you truly made them yours?

We are to hold tightly to the truth about the role of faith in a miracle. Our complete dependence on God—which we express when we take a risk of faith—makes more room for Him to act.

But there's still one enormous obstacle that prevents people from putting what they know about miracles into action. The tricky thing is, it looks exactly like fear. But it's not.

Getting to the root of fear

All of us feel fear when we're about to do something that involves considerable risk. Risk, after all, means there's no guarantee of success. And usually when we feel fear, we don't proceed.

But fear is a fruit, not the root. The root is unbelief in our hearts. That's why the greatest obstacle to a life marked by miracles is not fear but unbelief.

Unbelief is our unwillingness to believe that God is who He says He is and will do what He says He will do. When we respond with unbelief, we are saying to God, "You are not trustworthy. Therefore, if I'm faced with a situation that depends on You to come through, I won't take a risk."

Think about what unbelief looks like from God's perspective. It could be illustrated by the boy who refuses to jump into his father's arms because he believes his dad won't catch him—and may not even want to. Or by Peter refusing to get out of the boat because he believed that if he started to sink, Jesus would not reach out to save him. Or by any one of us who has been saved, blessed, protected, provided for, and comforted by our heavenly Father, only to tell Him, "Yes, You have done all those things and more for me, and I know that You have my best interests at heart, but I still don't trust You."

When the residents of Nazareth didn't have faith in Jesus despite observing His miracles firsthand, He "marveled because of their unbelief."[7] Why did Jesus marvel? Because they clung to their unbelief in the face of over-whelming evidence that they should have clung to faith.

The lesson for us is clear. We don't tear down unbelief in our hearts by trying to muster up our courage or fan the flames of emotion. We tear it down by rejecting the lies, claiming the truth, and acting on it. Then we take courage in spite of fear…and step out of the boat.

> *We don't tear down unbelief by trying to muster up our courage or fan the flames of emotion. We tear it down by rejecting the lies.*

You can take action today to move from un-belief to active faith by applying five simple but profound steps:

- Affirm that God is who He says He is.
- Admit to God that unbelief is sin, and apologize to Him for breaking faith in your relationship with Him.
- Recount and remember how God has come through in the past for you and for so many others in the Bible and history.
- Keep your eyes on Christ, not the circumstances you find your-self in or the feelings you are experiencing.
- Precommit to purposefully exercising risky faith whenever it is called for in the course of delivering a miracle.

With these actions, you are intentionally resting your hopes on the record, character, and promise of God. And you have signaled to Him that you are now a prime candidate to deliver a miracle.

The promise of risk

I hope you are beginning to grasp the indispensable part you and I play in whether or not a miracle will happen. The amount of our faith—and the actions we take as a result—can either limit or release God to act in a mira-cle situation.

The exhilarating promise of the Risk Key is that it enables us to successfully and repeatedly deliver miracles for Heaven to those who are in need. And each time we exercise our faith, it will grow. Of course, no single action of risky faith is easy. Which leads me to suggest Delivery Agent Rule #1 on Risky Faith: "If it's easy, I'm probably not taking a risk of faith." Followed, thankfully, by Delivery Agent Rule #2 on Risky Faith: "If my risk of faith is a little scary, I'm probably in line for a wonderful miracle."

I can tell you from years of personal experience that the proactive faith I've talked about in this chapter will radically change your life for the better…and you'll never want to go back. Paul encouraged the Thessalonians to take risks of faith when he prayed that "by His power" God would "fulfill every good purpose of yours and every act prompted by your faith."[8]

Every genuine act of faith expands your horizons for God. Before long you will find yourself actually looking for greater risk opportunities for Him because you know that the size of the risk also determines the size of the reward.

Part 3

———————⬥※⬥———————

HOW TO DELIVER
A MIRACLE

8

The Five Signals That Guide a Miracle Delivery

You were born to understand and respond to miracle-related signals

If you think about it, signals carrying important information come at you all day long, and you know what they mean. In fact, the message is so clear and helpful that you rarely stop to reflect on the signal:

- A man in a crowd waves his hand above his head. ("Look. Over here!")
- Your toddler bursts into tears while grabbing his knee. ("Mommy! Owee!")
- Red lights flash at a railroad crossing. A gate descends across your lane. ("Stop. Do not proceed.")
- You're standing in line for concert tickets when you feel a tap on your arm. ("Hey!")
- You ask your teen, "Where were you?" He looks down. (Uh-oh.)

Since we're talking in this book about partnering with God to deliver His miracles to others, wouldn't it be wonderful if you and I could count on the same kind of unmistakable, universally identifiable signals to guide us in our work for God?

The good news is, we can. Miracle-specific signals are being sent our way on a regular basis, and we can learn to read and respond to them. These messages have always been there. And even though most of us routinely miss them, they are messages that sent ones must learn to recognize and respond to in order to cooperate with God for miracle outcomes.

Miracle-specific signals are being sent our way on a regular basis, and we can learn to read and respond to them.

In this book I identify five miracle-related signals: a *nudge,* a *cue,* a *bump,* a *prompt,* and an *alert.* You may have already noticed passing references to them. But now it's time to slow down, define them, and show how they work.

Using such simple terms to describe what the Spirit is up to in our world will probably be a new experience for you. But I promise you'll discover right away that putting miracle-related signals to work is not difficult. You'll realize you already know more than you think. You just may not have named or defined what's happening until now. You'll find yourself saying, "I already do that!" or, "That makes complete sense!"

Once you put them to work in your partnership with God, your success rate as an agent for the miraculous will rapidly increase. You will experience the exhilaration of being truly alive to what God is doing in the Everyday Miracle Territory.

Unfortunately, common misconceptions in this area limit success. For example, most people assume that signals surrounding a miracle event must be too mysterious for an ordinary person to decode.

But that's not true. We serve a God who has gone to extraordinary lengths to communicate with us. He even sent His Son to earth with a message from Heaven. And today He makes His way known to us through the Bible, through His Spirit, and in other ways as we walk in daily dependence on Him to lead and guide. Of course, understanding what God intends for us at a specific moment won't be like getting a text message from a friend or seeing your name written in the sky. But God intends to connect, and He does. For example, God told Isaiah,

> *Your ears shall hear a word behind you, saying,*
> *"This is the way, walk in it,"*
> *Whenever you turn to the right hand*
> *Or whenever you turn to the left.*[1]

God wants to and will guide and direct us—all the more so when we are committed to partnering with Him in the tasks He cares about most.

Another common misconception concerns how people communicate. Many assume that only the highly trained can read the verbal and nonverbal signals people send about what they really think and feel. But the fact is, we all do this already. The pages ahead are packed with examples.

The five signals help you navigate your way to and through the miracle God wants you to be a part of. For example, they help you

- identify the specific person God has in mind for your miracle appointment,
- determine which of the person's needs is the one God wants you to focus on,
- know when you are succeeding in opening someone's heart to receive a miracle,
- feel confident that God is leading you even when you are unsure,
- know how to interpret your own thoughts and emotions,

- receive and respond to miracle-specific information that comes
  to you from God and others.

Let's begin with a story.

Richard and April's story

It was early morning. Richard had to catch a flight. But in his rush to get to the airport, he left behind one of those little things that are so easy to forget: his cell phone charger.

"On the way to the airport, I swung by the office to pick it up," he told me. "But it was before six, and the alarm system was still on. I stopped the car. Should I try to deactivate, then reactivate the system just for my phone cord? I was envisioning the alarm going off, the whole neighborhood waking up, police, missing my flight. I turned around and headed for the airport."

At his connecting airport in Dallas, Richard bought another charger for his phone. While he was waiting for his next flight, he walked the concourse, praying, *Lord, is there anyone You want me to meet here?*

Walking toward the store where he had earlier bought the charger, he noticed the salesperson who had helped him, standing by the store entrance. Richard was well past her when he had an unexpected thought: *Lord, that's the young lady You want me to talk to, isn't it?* He hadn't even considered that idea when he was making his purchase.

So Richard said to God, *If she's still standing there when I go back*—which would mean no customers in the store—*I'll talk to her.*

"Well, when I went back, there she still was, leaning against the glass window," said Richard. "I said, 'Hi, I'm the guy who bought the charger. I just called my wife.'"

"That's good," she told him with a smile. He introduced himself. Her name was April.

Richard hesitated. He sensed a pang of uncertainty about what he felt led to say next. Should he proceed in faith? He made his decision.

"April, may I ask you a question?" he asked.

"Sure."

"If you could wish for one thing from God today, what would that be?"

April's eyes suddenly brimmed with tears. "My baby is coming in three months!" Richard didn't understand, but he instantly sensed God telling him, *She needs you to pray for her.*

Tearfully, April placed her hand on her stomach. "The doctor says the baby may be born with serious health problems."

"You must feel very afraid. May I say a short prayer for you right now?"

"Oh, would you? I know God sent you!"

"Do you know the Lord, April?" When she said yes, he explained. "I want you to know that I was walking up and down this concourse asking the Lord if there was anyone He wanted me to meet here. It is you, isn't it?"

"Yes, it is!"

While people came and went around them, Richard prayed, asking God to comfort April, grant her a safe delivery, and allow her baby to be born healthy. When he was done, she seemed encouraged and calm. He told her that since he was coming back to the airport in a few days, he'd like to stop by and see how she was doing.

April said she'd love that. "Thank you so much. I know God sent you to me today."

Elated that God had led him so clearly, Richard headed to the gate to catch his flight. Suddenly it dawned on him just how God had brought the two of them together. *Lord,* he prayed, *You did not want me to go back to the office and get my phone cord, did You? Thanks for leading me to meet April.*

Surfacing the signals

I share Richard's story because it's a good example of how a sent person who's paying attention to the signals can connect with the one person God wants to touch through him. With a little practice, you can recognize the subtle clues in a story like Richard's that make it more than an inspiring account of someone's good deed. Without these turning points, no miracle would have occurred.

Let's retrace what happened:

- Richard, a man in a hurry, leaves home in Atlanta (oops, forgot something). About the same time, April, a fearful young mother, heads to work in Dallas.
- Now in Dallas, Richard paces the airport, asking God to send him to a person in need.
- God in Heaven, intent on reassuring April, signals Richard— *That's the one. See her standing there?* In this book we call that a **nudge.**
- Before he asks his question, Richard feels suddenly uncertain, a little anxious. In this book we call that an **alert.**
- Richard asks April a question that opens her heart. In this book we call that a **bump.**
- April signals Richard: she bursts into tears and shares her need. In this book we call that a **cue.**
- God signaled Richard that April needed his prayer. In this book we call that a **prompt.** The source of a prompt is our unseen partner, the Holy Spirit.
- April experiences personal proof that God knows and cares about her and her baby. In this book we call that a successful delivery! (More about this in the next chapter.)
- Her despair relieved, she tells Richard, "God sent you to me!" Richard agrees. Without God, the whole thing wouldn't have happened. In this book we call that transferring the credit. (More about this in the next chapter too.)

In this brief exchange between total strangers, you can see all five signals we'll talk about: a nudge, a cue, a bump, a prompt, and an alert. Taken together, these signals help us find and accomplish the miracle work God has in mind.

If you haven't already, you'll soon realize how simple and intuitive these signals are. That's good news for all of us average folks who want to be part of extraordinary God-incidents on a regular basis.

Let's take a closer look at each.

_____ Signal 1 _____

The God Nudge

How Heaven gets your attention and provides direction

A nudge is an inner push that directs us toward a person, a place, or an action. It is a signal from God that, no matter how faint, suddenly turns our attention to something or someone we weren't thinking about.

God nudged Richard to see the salesclerk in a different light—as an appointment God had waiting for him. Nudges are almost always about a single act that God wants done soon.

The nudge might direct us toward a person in our line of sight. I call that a *visual nudge.* Our eyes are drawn to a person in a way that feels as if God is highlighting his presence, and we sense there might be an underlying reason. Most of us know very well what this experience is like. We just need to become aware of how often it happens.

> *A nudge is an inner push that directs us toward a person, a place, or an action.*

More often we experience what I call a *non-visual nudge,* which means the person we're prompted to think about isn't around. You may have described this experience before with words like "I felt God leading me toward…" or "Out of nowhere Aunt Iris came to mind."

A nudge is simply one way God communicates His wishes to our minds.

On rare occasions He also uses dreams, visions, angels, and other individuals. But the most common kind of communication is a small, interrupting thought to get our attention: *Call Aunt Iris.*

Of course, not every interrupting thought is from God. I don't mistake my sudden craving for cherry cobbler as a signal from Heaven. Still, we can and must become skilled at discerning and interpreting God's unique style of guidance.

Most of God's guidance is without words. In case you wonder if something is wrong with you, I assure you that few people hear God audibly. As we've already acknowledged, He makes His general leading known to us through His Word, His Spirit, other people, and our thoughts and feelings. As you've already seen demonstrated in this book, Heaven has no problem communicating with us, even if it is without words.

Regardless of the way God's nudges are communicated, they tend to have certain qualities in common.

A nudge is unexpected and out of context. Typically, you're not on your knees in prayer asking God to nudge you. Instead, you're driving to work or brushing your teeth when it comes: *Go talk to that man,* or *Stop here.* It's unexpected and out of context. A God nudge rarely comes in the middle of your thoughts about a given person, place, or event but rather interrupts your thoughts about something else. God wants it to be clear: *This thought isn't yours but Mine!*

A nudge is subtle but clear. God doesn't mumble, but then again, He rarely shouts. This means His nudge is clear enough that we have no doubt we received the message. We often wish it were more complete, had more details. But where information or an explanation is missing, God wants us to exercise faith and act on what we have received.

A nudge is uncomfortable. A nudge invites you to do something you don't want to do. That's another reason it is so easy to dismiss. We commonly rationalize, "If God is asking me to do something, I will always feel great peace about it." But the truth is often just the opposite. God's work almost always requires that we stop what we're doing or what we have planned and make His agenda our priority. That's why He's looking for volunteers who will say yes regardless of discomfort or inconvenience.

Discerning the nudge is a learned skill. A God nudge will always bear fruit. If a nudge I follow doesn't lead to a positive result, then I know to pay closer attention the next time.

Once you're sure you've experienced a nudge from God, act on it as soon as possible. Some of the saddest stories I've heard are from people who brushed off nudges from God, only to discover later that He was directing them toward a miracle appointment with someone in desperate straits.

Signal 2

The Revealing Cue
How people reveal a need God may want to meet through you

While a nudge comes from God, a cue is a signal that comes from another person. It is communicated, often unknowingly, by someone's words or body language. In the case of the person you're connecting with for a miracle, cues will convey important information about how he's feeling, what he wants, how emotionally open or closed he is, and most important, what needs he may have at the time.

> *A cue is communicated, often unknowingly, by someone's words or body language.*

A cue can come as more of a shout than a whisper. How could Richard miss the fact that April had just burst into tears? And she didn't just start crying. She told Richard exactly what was bothering her.

More often than not, though, a cue is fleeting. It's easy to overlook or disregard. We have to reach out and capture it.

Cues come in two ways. A *verbal cue* conveys a message in words. A *body language cue* conveys a message through a person's posture, facial expressions, or gestures. Taken together, the two kinds of cues often present a more complete picture of what a person is feeling and thinking.

We all know more about cues than we realize. Take smiles. A smile is not just a smile, is it? One kind of smile tells us a person is happy. Another—say, a quick or forced smile that doesn't reach the eyes—means something else altogether. And the smile of a person in pain? That's difficult to explain, but we know it when we see it.

Without realizing it, all of us send out cues constantly. We telegraph to others whether we're friendly or hostile, paying attention or daydreaming, relaxed or feeling defensive, along with dozens of other emotions. Just as constantly, people around us pick up on them. Or they don't.

Give thought to the following cues and the needs they reveal:

- A teen girl, her face drained of color, gasps, "I can't believe she did that!" She feels shock now. What comes next might be hurt, anger, or betrayal.
- A dad stares at the floor and says sadly, "I'm not sure that my son even wants me to come." Is he feeling rejected? discouraged? like a failure?
- A female co-worker slouches in her chair and exclaims, "Why do these things keep happening to me?" She feels defeated. Life hasn't been fair.
- An elderly man stands by a window. He's holding a little dog like it's his last friend in the world. "I haven't been the same since my wife died," he tells you. His feelings are right at the surface, and his cues suggest he might feel lonely, abandoned, afraid, or angry.

Our ability to read and respond to cues, as with nudges, is learned. Salespeople, trial attorneys, counselors, diplomats, and people in social services—

to name a few—take reading cues very seriously. They constantly strive to improve their ability to read them. Once you and I sign up to deliver miracles for God, we need to do the same. Fortunately, we don't need special training. We can easily find a crash course on the Web or in our nearest bookstore. Or just sit in a coffee shop or mall and practice people watching.

In fact, you can practice reading cues anytime you're around other people. Focus on how particular words, movements, and postures work together to instantly communicate a wealth of information. Train yourself especially to listen for words and phrases that convey emotion:

- "I'm so worried that…"
- "I wish that…"
- "I can't believe that…"
- "I should never have…"

If you keep at it, the day will come when you'll be able to read what ails a person's soul with surprising accuracy.

But what if the signals seem absent or those we get are confusing? Do we conclude that the other person doesn't have a need? Since we know that at all times and in all places everyone has a need that God wants to meet, it makes sense to be ready with a proactive step. That brings us to our third practical tool for detecting a personal need.

Signal 3

The Clarifying Bump

How you use a question to clarify a person's need

A bump is something you do to another person to surface or confirm a need. A bump is usually a question. Richard surfaced April's need with a bump: "If you could wish for one thing from God today, what would that be?"

As with a cue, the purpose of a bump is to help us gain more insight into a person's need. We gently gather the needed information by asking the right questions. The person's answer or reaction will point us to the need that God desires us to meet in partnership with Him.

With the first two signals, we are receivers. With the bump, we are initiators. An easy way to think about the first three signals is this:

- A nudge comes to you from God.
- A cue comes to you from another person.
- A bump goes from you to another person.

The purpose of a bump is to help us gain more insight into a person's need.

As with nudges and cues, bumps are already part of our lives. We bump someone every time we ask, "How are you doing?" or "You okay?" The difference with a miracle-related bump is that we really want to know, because we're on a mission. We're looking for specific information that clarifies our understanding of a person's need.

A bump is not an intrusion or a question out of the blue. We don't suddenly have permission to be socially inappropriate. For example, you wouldn't walk up to a couple you don't know and ask how their marriage is going.

An effective bump is often based on information you've already gathered either by observation (nonverbal cues) or by careful listening (verbal cues). You're in a doctor's office waiting room. You notice that a mom with three young children looks exhausted. You catch her attention. "It must be stressful to wait for the doctor with several kids in tow," you say empathetically. "How do you manage?"

Might any thoughtful person ask the same question? Sure. The difference is, you're on a mission. You're looking for an opportunity for a miracle you can deliver.

The best bumps tend to be open-ended questions that can't be answered with a simple yes or no. This invites the person to share more helpful information.

In *The Prayer of Jabez,* I wrote about my favorite bump: "How may I help you?" I often call it the Elisha bump because the biblical prophet Elisha asked a similar question three times, and miracles followed each time.[2]

Here are some other clarifying bumps:

- "If you could change something about your life, what would it be?"
- What are one or two of the biggest problems your family is facing these days?
- If you could ask God one question, what would it be?
- What, if anything, has discouraged you lately?
- If Jesus were standing here, what do you think He'd say about this discussion?

The more you practice, the easier bumps will become. You'll learn how to phrase a question sensitively and specifically for the person at hand. Just remember to keep your bumps gentle, inviting, and purposeful.

And your purpose is simple. You are asking to be invited into the inner place where a personal miracle is completed—the heart.

Reading Signs in the Desert
Nudges, cues, and bumps in the Bible

If God can bring Richard and April together from different states for a miracle, do you think He could bring together two people from different continents for a miracle, using the same nudges, cues, and bumps we've just talked about...and leave a record of it in the Bible?

You might have read in the Bible about Philip's encounter with an

African official, but I'm guessing you never noticed the signals that brought it all together. I've included the story here, inserting a few comments about signals to show you what I mean.

The miracle encounter, found in Acts 8:26–39, begins with a very unusual nudge, and things get only more exciting from there.

> **Whopper nudge:** *An angel of the Lord spoke to Philip, saying, "Arise and go toward the south along the road which goes down from Jerusalem to Gaza." This is desert. So he arose and went.*

> **Cue:** *And behold, a man of Ethiopia, a eunuch of great authority under Candace the queen of the Ethiopians, who had charge of all her treasury, and had come to Jerusalem to worship, was returning. And sitting in his chariot,...*

> **Big cue:** *...he was reading Isaiah the prophet.*

In just three verses Philip has responded to a nudge and left town. Where to? He's not sure. *Just start walking toward the desert.* But surely as he walks along that road, he's giving every passerby a careful look. "Why do You want me here, Lord?" he asks. "Is there someone here You want me to meet?" Then a chariot approaches, one that stands out from all the rest. Clearly, the man inside is a VIP. *Hmmm.* And he's reading the Bible? *That must be the person!*

> **Nudge:** *Then the Spirit said to Philip, "Go near and overtake this chariot."*

> **Bump:** *So Philip ran to him, and heard him reading the prophet Isaiah, and said, "Do you understand what you are reading?"*

Nice leading question, don't you think? Friendly Philip. No wonder Philip's bump worked perfectly. Look at what happens next.

> **Another big cue:** *And he said, "How can I, unless someone guides me?" And he asked Philip to come up and sit with him. The place in the Scripture which he read was this:*

> *"He was led as a sheep to the slaughter;*
> *And as a lamb before its shearer is silent,*
> *So He opened not His mouth.*
> *In His humiliation His justice was taken away,*
> *And who will declare His generation?*
> *For His life is taken from the earth."*

> **And another big cue:** *So the eunuch answered Philip and said, "I ask you, of whom does the prophet say this, of himself or of some other man?" Then Philip opened his mouth, and beginning at this Scripture, preached Jesus to him. Now as they went down the road, they came to some water.*

> **And yet another big cue:** *And the eunuch said, "See, here is water. What hinders me from being baptized?"*

But wait. Do you see what's really happening here? Philip is at work following God's nudges and using a bump. But behind the scenes is the real action. The Holy Spirit is powerfully at work in the Ethiopian's heart. We know that because his cues are constant and increasingly urgent. He literally begs Philip to help him find the miracle of salvation.

Philip asks just one more question—to validate the Ethiopian's sincerity—and the encounter reaches its climax.

Bump: *Then Philip said, "If you believe with all your heart, you may."*

Miracle delivered: *And he answered and said, "I believe that Jesus Christ is the Son of God." So he commanded the chariot to stand still. And both Philip and the eunuch went down into the water, and he baptized him.*

I hope you encountered this miracle story in an entirely different way than you have in the past. Surfacing the signals helps us become better students of what God cares so passionately about—delivering His saving goodness and power to people.

I also hope you see that the signals I'm describing are simply helpful tools to point out how miracle messages happen in normal life. I also hope you see why they're so important to understand and use in our partnership with God.

Now I want to show you the fourth important signal.

_____ *Signal 4* ____

The Spirit Prompt
How God provides you with insight during the delivery of a miracle

A prompt is a signal from God to you in the form of a sudden insight about the person you are seeking to help. The purpose of a prompt is to reveal information you could not otherwise know in order to help you deliver a miracle. Prompts usually occur while you're talking with a person (unlike nudges, which happen at the front end and help you identify your miracle appointment).

A prompt has much in common with a nudge, but the differences are important:

- A nudge is *directional.* God directs your attention toward a person or a place so you will connect with your miracle appointment.
- A prompt is *informational.* God drops into your thoughts a nugget of information about the person or situation that better enables you to deliver the miracle.

Thankfully, there is nothing spooky or magical about a prompt, even though it supernaturally links Heaven and earth. In fact, a prompt happens so quickly that you may not realize until later that you received one and were acting on it. Later you may wonder, *Where did that thought come from?*

A prompt is a sudden insight about the person you are seeking to help.

At other times a prompt is more challenging. It may not make sense immediately, or it may convey something that can push you beyond your comfort zone:

- *Why should I ask about her grandfather when we're talking about her marriage?*
- *Why should I tell him to make his bed?* (Remember Jimmy in chapter 1?)

In such instances you may feel tentative, uncomfortable, or even afraid. Why? Because you're being challenged to trust the information you're receiving. It requires you to take a step of faith, demonstrating that you trust the Spirit's guidance and His intentions.

That's why fear at such a point is rarely, if ever, a sign for you to turn back. The real purpose of fear is to alert you that a risk of faith is in order. (We look at the surprising usefulness of alerts in Signal 5.)

I just mentioned Jimmy from chapter 1. As you recall, he was talking to Nick, a man who desperately wanted to save his marriage. When Nick asked

Jimmy what he should do, Jimmy was nervous. That's why he told Nick to get paper and pen—he was stalling because he didn't know what to say. And then God put the prompt in Jimmy's mind: *Tell Nick he should go home and make his bed.*

So the point is this: even though Jimmy was hesitant to say something he couldn't defend, he kept going, and God came through for both men, His miraculous hand clearly evident. Nick exclaimed, "How did you know?" Because Jimmy trusted God enough to say what he did, Nick knew that God was intervening and cared about him and his marriage.

This next story is another helpful example because it was clearly initiated by a nudge, then the need was suggested by a prompt. Here's what happened.

One morning Toni asked God to send her to do His work that day. One hour later she noticed something ordinarily she would have missed. She was in a meeting when a woman she didn't know well made a passing comment about sons being a challenge. Something in her remark alerted Toni to a hidden ache.

"I don't think anyone else in the room noticed anything," she recalls. When Toni asked God to show her how she could help, she felt a clear nudge. It came in the form of a direction: *Write her a note.*

Toni didn't have much to go on. But she took out a pad and pen.

Dear Sonya, your son is in a...

What was she going to say? She didn't know.
Then God prompted her. A picture came into Toni's mind.

...wrestling match with God. He's fighting hard, but it won't be long till he goes limp. God is going to hold him tight till he gives up completely. It will be the love of God that wins.

When Toni was done, she folded the note, wrote Sonya's name on it, and passed it down the row. She noticed that when Sonya opened the note, she began to quietly weep. Toni thought, *Oh no! Maybe I got it all wrong.*

But as soon as the meeting ended, Sonya came up to Toni with a question. "How did you know?"

"How did I know what?"

"My son is a wrestler. He loves to wrestle," she said, still tearful.

Then she told the rest of the story. "You're right. Lately he's been wrestling with God. In fact, in just one hour he'll be standing before a judge on an assault charge. My husband and I can't be there to help him, so we've been praying that God will be his advocate in that courtroom."

The women decided to go to lunch. Then just as their sandwiches arrived, the woman's son called. The court had dismissed the charge. "I know God was watching out for me," he told his mom. "I get a chance to start over—and I'm going to."

Isn't it reassuring that God *wants* to communicate with us when we serve Him? As you awaken your spiritual senses to what God is showing you, you can rest in the fact that God will lead you into the most meaningful experiences of your life so far. More and more, you'll experience a spiritual peace that confirms you are heading in the right direction.

Here's something else to consider: during the miracle delivery process, inner peace and surface anxiety will often coexist. You can be anxious about a prompt yet still experience peace and confidence that God's Spirit is at work through you.

And remember, a prompt is to help you deliver the miracle. It's not a revelation about the future or a message for another person. (For example, you won't find yourself saying, "God told me to tell you...") Rather, a prompt is an insight or information God gives you to act on in the moment so you can complete your miracle assignment with excellence.

The Fear Alert

How we signal ourselves when to go forward in faith

A fear alert is a signal you receive from yourself. During a delivery the alert is a reliable indicator from your emotions that you should exercise your faith and move *through* your feelings toward the miracle.

A fear alert is a reliable indicator that you should exercise your faith.

Let's talk first about fear itself. Fear is like the warning light on your car dashboard; it tells you, "Pay attention!" We experience this normal human emotion in varying degrees many times a day, such as when we're trying to maneuver through rush-hour traffic, when we've been unexpectedly called into our boss's office, or when we realize we forgot to pay an important bill and the power may be turned off by the time we get home.

A fear alert occurs during the process of a miracle delivery because you are no longer in your comfort zone. You are taking a risk of faith. Since miracles rarely happen inside a delivery agent's comfort zone, a fear alert is actually full of promise and serves as a very different kind of warning light: "Pay attention! Exercise your faith! Miracle directly ahead!"

Of course, if you verbalized a fear alert to yourself, it might sound like this:

- "Who, me? I can't possibly be the right person to deliver this miracle!"
- "Do what? I can't succeed at that!"
- "What will they think? I will get ridiculed and rejected if I say that!"

Once we identify what's happening, we can be proactive about our response—and what we do next makes all the difference. Of course the human mind and body use fear signals to keep us away from danger. But in our work of partnering with God for a miracle, the very same alerts can become something else: *confirmation* that we are moving in the right direction (toward a miracle) and an *invitation* to overcome fear with faith.

This kind of active trust in God's Spirit is foundational to a lifestyle of predictable miracles because it activates the partnership and makes room for God to do what only He can do: the miracle. Instead of responding to fear in the normal way—by fleeing or postponing—you purposefully interpret the alert as a valuable signal that it's now time for you to exercise your faith and complete the very action you're afraid to do.

Take a second look at the story that opens chapter 2. I was in the middle of speaking to eighty men at a conference when I received a clear and very specific nudge. God wanted me to ask a man sitting four rows back on the aisle what I could do for him. I paused, walked down the aisle, and asked, "Sir, I feel like there is something unusual going on in your life. Is there anything I can do for you?"

I don't usually behave that way when I'm addressing an audience! Every step down the aisle, I was feeling uncomfortable, awkward, a little foolish. The man's reply didn't help. He told me in no uncertain terms that he was just fine, thank you very much.

I retraced my steps to the podium feeling even more uncomfortable, awkward, and foolish. But I had just picked up my comments where I'd left off when God nudged me again and even more dramatically.

This time the fear and discomfort alarm in my heart really went off! What was God doing? Hadn't I already tried that once without success? The men in the audience had flown in from all over the country to hear me speak on a particular topic. What would they think if I made a fool of myself again and wasted even more of their time?

I experienced fear alerts all over the place. But for sent ones intent on doing what God wants done, a fear alert is not a signal to turn back but a signal to step forward. I decided to stop speaking and walk down that aisle again and—depending on God for a miracle—ask that man the same question a second time. The result was a huge miracle that radically altered the weekend for the entire audience and showed all of us in an unforgettable way the wonders of God's love and power.

More than with any other signal, misinterpretations of the fear alert short-circuit the miracle process. But it doesn't have to be that way. Fear and discomfort are just negative emotions. We shouldn't wait until those feelings go away but rather act in faith in spite of them. We don't have to blindly obey what they push us to do. Instead, we can look past our feelings and press forward to the miracle that is waiting to happen.

I've identified the most common times during a miracle delivery when your fear-alert caution light is likely to start flashing. For a helpful discussion on these, along with a summary chart of all five signals, go to www.You WereBornForThis.com.

"Now I can understand and use miracle-related signals"

When I first present these simple truths about miracle-specific signals to audiences, I notice two predictable cues.

One is heads nodding. That's body language for "Absolutely! You're right. That *is* the way it works." Many come up to me later and confirm that I've read the cue correctly.

The other, which comes later in the session, is people staring thoughtfully into space, sometimes with their eyes closed. Or they'll look down pensively. I know from hearing from them later what that cue means too. It's body language for "O Lord, I must have missed hundreds of miracle opportunities that You have constantly, purposefully, lovingly brought my way…but I didn't recognize and respond to the signals."

What cue are you sending right now?

If you're sobered by what you might have missed, let me remind you of something: now that you know how signals work, your life can begin to change today. Reading signals from God, others, and yourself as they relate to a personal miracle is a natural and immediately usable skill.

I hope you've seen the promise of learning to recognize, receive, and send miracle-related messages. That's what you were born to do. God created you to partner with Him in a process that produces memorable miracle outcomes.

The result of your learning to read miracle-related signals will be astonishment, gratitude, and glory to God. The book of Acts says that after Philip and the Ethiopian parted, the official "went on his way rejoicing."[3]

You will too.

———————————————— ⋯✣⋯ ————————————————

9

The Five Steps That Lead to a Miracle Delivery

*You were born to know and follow
miracle-related delivery steps*

*A*t the *beginning* of this book, I proposed that God chooses to partner with ordinary people for His supernatural agenda. For such an extraordinary role, I said, no previous experience was required. No special degree, talent, or qualification either.

But for that to be true, wouldn't there have to be skills we could learn and an approach that would bring success—not just once but regularly—in our new life in Everyday Miracle Territory? Of course, Heaven's part in delivering miracles would still be full of mystery, just as you'd expect, but our part would have to be very down-to-earth.

Thankfully, a simple, self-evident approach to delivering miracles does exist. In fact, the ideas can be understood by a ten-year-old. And why wouldn't that be the case if delivering personal miracles is part of God's agenda for each of us? How else could we explain the fact that God has been using people to deliver personal miracles for centuries?

The process I want to teach you begins with the five parts of every personal miracle. These parts are present even if we can't see them. If you were to revisit the stories you've encountered so far to identify elements that always appear, I think you'd come up with a similar list.

For a personal miracle to take place, we must have

- a person (the recipient of the miracle),
- a need (the purpose for any personal miracle),
- an open heart (the place where a personal miracle is completed),
- a delivery agent (the means for getting the miracle where it is needed),
- God (the Person who *does* the miracle and receives the credit).

As motivated delivery agents, we can get from these basic elements of a miracle to a job description in no time. For example, the five parts suggest a series of steps we can follow to partner with God successfully. The steps are universal, learnable, repeatable, and aligned with how Heaven actually works in a miracle situation. I call them the Five Steps for Delivering Personal Miracles:

1. Identify the person.
2. Isolate the need.
3. Open the heart.
4. Deliver the miracle.
5. Transfer the credit.

When we put these elements in the order in which most miracles unfold, we have a set of action steps that we can learn and use. For the miracles we focus on in this chapter, a step sometimes appears to get skipped or the order of steps unfolds differently. But I think the reasons for this will be clear to you as we look at them together. What you can count on is that all five steps play an important role in every personal miracle.

In the next section of the book, which deals with three special delivery miracles, the sequence of the steps becomes even more important. When taken in order, they will help you guide a conversation toward a specific, known miracle outcome.

Don't think of these steps as a rigid formula but as a basic framework. My goal is to be helpful without diminishing in any way the grandeur and leadership of God in the process.

You'll see that the five-step pattern brings together all the big ideas you've learned so far: now you are a *sent person* (Master Key) who *shares God's heart for people* (People Key) and who *intentionally partners with the Spirit* to do God's work (Spirit Key) through *acts of proactive dependence on Him* (Risk Key) in delivering His miracle to others.

My intention is to describe what I've learned through Bible study, extensive research, and personal experience over many years so you can deliver miracles for God in increasing numbers in your life.

_____ *Step 1* ____

Identify the Person

If God is going to meet a specific need for another person through us, then we need to find and connect with that person. That's step number one. To put it in delivery agent terms, we begin by asking, "Where am I taking this package? Who is it for?"

One of the best ways to find our answer is to respond to God's nudges. A nudge directs us to that special person who will be our appointment.

With Owen, I received a very specific nudge not once but twice. In my experience, God generally doesn't repeat a nudge

> *To put it in delivery agent terms, we ask, "Where am I taking this package? Who is it for?"*

if we willfully ignore it. But if we genuinely need further guidance, He may nudge us again.

The fact that a nudge seems out of context or surprises us is a help in identifying our person with confidence:

- *Give the waiter one hundred dollars.* (my encounter with Jack)
- *Show Marta My heart for her.* (Lauren and Marta's story)
- *Look. The woman from the phone store.* (Richard and April's story)

As the stories in this book demonstrate, God leads us to appointments in different ways. But a process that might sound vague to a person who doesn't understand miracle missions shouldn't sound vague to you by now. You see the world very differently than you used to. Where before you saw a waiter, a co-worker, or a neighbor, you now see people with needs—needs often known only to God, needs that He may want to meet today through you.

Sometimes we'll assume an encounter is about one thing, only to suddenly realize, *Oh! God has something else in mind.* Sometimes the person finds us and declares in so many words that he desperately needs a miracle. Think back to Jimmy in chapter 1. His first clue that Nick might be a miracle appointment came when Nick started talking about his troubled marriage.

I always encourage people who are just getting started with delivering Heaven's miracles not to get hung up on wondering, *Is this the person?* in every conversation. You don't make your miracle appointment; God brings it to you through His nudge, through causing you to see their cues, or through your initiation by means of a bump.

Especially during your early days as a delivery agent, God will make your appointment obvious. Your job is simply to grow into your new role as Heaven's ambassador and to be awake to Heaven's agenda for your day.

In the meantime you're not doing anything socially unacceptable if you approach a person and start a conversation. If in doubt, proceed—all you risk is being friendly.

Step 2

Isolate the Need

Of all the possible needs the person you've identified may have (and we all have many needs), you now need to isolate the *specific need* God wants to meet through you at this time. Remember, God isn't asking you or me to meet every need or even necessarily to meet a person's greatest need. We're looking for the need that is at the top of God's agenda for us and for the person we've identified.

Of course, sometimes you can't miss the need. But more often it takes a little sleuthing to uncover the urgent need God wants to meet. As we discussed in the previous chapter, a lot of information about needs is signaled to us by tone of voice, body posture, circumstance, expression

> _We're looking for the need that is at the top of God's agenda for us and for the person we've identified._

of emotion, and words. We have described this as watching for cues—verbal and nonverbal messages that show or suggest what's happening inside the person.

Bumps also help to surface the need or to confirm that you have identified the right need. This is where a bump question like "How may I help you?" can be effective. You are taking a risk to make yourself available, depending on God to be at work in the other person so that he or she reveals the need God wants to meet through you. The best bump gets you past all the chatter, posturing, and surface conversation to focus directly on the need.

In my interaction with Owen, after two strong nudges it was clear to me that I had the right person. But getting Owen to open up about his need was challenging, to say the least. I bumped him in a personal and direct but open-ended way: "I sense that something is deeply troubling you." It wasn't until I risked a second bump that Owen's story, including his need, came tumbling out. Now I understood his crisis and had information that helped me steer him toward the miracle God wanted.

Of course God can work through us when specifics about the need are few or absent. You've probably already experienced this. You did something for another person without realizing that God was in it, and when you did, the recipient said, "I can't believe you did that. I've been asking God for that very thing!"

But what God *can* do doesn't change our responsibility in this step—to surface the need He wants to meet. Our role is to look for the need patiently and sensitively. More information can suddenly show you what God wants to do or why God chose you for the encounter. You're still relying on God's guidance, but now you can partner with Him more completely to meet the need at hand.

I've noticed that when I have the right need in view, I feel a sense of peace. Still, I often confirm that I have the correct one by asking the other person, "Is this need the one area that's bothering you most right now?" If it turns out that another need is the real one, I don't hesitate to switch focus.

Here's a practical reminder: if a glaring need surfaces in a conversation that we *can* meet with our own resources, we should respond. It's never right to ask how we can help if we have no intention of helping unless God does a miracle. James warned us against falling into this sort of smug spiritual detachment:

> *If a brother or sister is naked and destitute of daily food, and one of you says to them, "Depart in peace, be warmed and filled," but you do not give them the things which are needed for the body, what does it profit?*[1]

Now you're ready for the third delivery step, which goes to the place where a personal miracle is completed: a person's heart.

Step 3

Open the Heart

When it comes to personal miracles, the heart is where the action is. How often Jesus reached past a surface request to the deeper human need—for relationship, forgiveness, a sense of meaning, salvation. Yes, a miracle often does involve some kind of material provision. So by all means feed the hungry and clothe the naked, but miracle delivery agents don't stop there. We want to partner with God to get inside their heart. Only when a provision changes how the recipient sees and responds to God is the personal miracle complete.

Not surprisingly, our role in preparing another's heart to receive what God wants to do is a critical part of the delivery process. We want the person to let us in, to show us what really matters, in some cases to acknowledge with us that the need is real.

> _When it comes to personal miracles, the heart is where the action is._

Do you remember in chapter 2 how tightly Owen's heart was clamped shut? In my recounting of what happened, I didn't detail all my responses. But while Owen poured out his reasons for quitting ministry, I was actually very responsive:

- To show him that I empathized with his pain, I slowly nodded in agreement and said softly, "I understand."
- To let him know that I was actively listening, that I really did care, I responded with "Hmmm"—the universal word for "I'm right with you!"
- To show him my acceptance of him as a person, my body posture was open and relaxed, not rigid and judgmental. I tilted my head to the side to let him know that I was concentrating on genuine understanding.

In other words, I was both sincere and intentional. In fact, if I hadn't already identified Owen as a miracle appointment and purposed to draw out his heart, things might have proceeded very differently. For example, I simply might have encouraged Owen to reconsider his plan to quit his ministry, or I might have asked the other men to remember him in their prayers—both caring, Christian responses, you'll agree, but not very helpful in opening his heart. And, without his heart open, a miracle in the making might have been thwarted.

Note that I wasn't trying to change Owen's mind about anything. I was simply doing my part and believing the Spirit was doing His part to prepare Owen's heart for the miracle I was now convinced God had brought me to deliver.

Opening a heart can happen naturally, with almost no effort. As we've seen in several stories, sometimes people throw their heart wide open to you as soon as their need is isolated. This is especially the case when they are in a lot of pain and the emotions are already near the surface. I think that before my friend Richard had even finished his bump ("If you could wish for one thing from God today…"), April's emotions were already rising to the surface.

But if a heart seems closed, how do you open it? We know we can't force it open. A heart tends to respond best to gentle and sincere invitations from the heart of another. Here are some tips on how to speak the powerful, universal language of the heart (some I've already shown in my conversation with Owen):

- *Maintain eye contact.* Eyes really are the windows to the soul.
- *Soften and lower your voice.* We talk about our feelings at a slower pace, with a deeper tone, and at a softer volume than we use to debate ideas, discuss the news, or tell jokes.
- *Slow down and practice pausing.* In this way, you're inviting the other person to carry more of the conversation. You're saying, "What you have to say is very important."

- *Relax your posture.* Our bodies speak volumes without words. So make sure your posture and gestures are conveying openness and safety. You sincerely want to be invited into the other person's most protected place—his or her heart.

- *Invite more heart sharing.* A head tilted to the side indicates you are in a listening mood. A quiet "Hmmm" shows you're really paying attention and you care. Nods indicate you understand and are interested. When a verbal response is in order, use a gentle bump like "How does that make you feel?" or "What does your heart tell you at a moment like this?" Or even use a straightforward question: "What is happening in your heart right now?"

- *Practice empathy.* Empathy means you put yourself in the other person's shoes. In the Master Key chapter, I told you about my encounter with a man in need alongside the freeway who had been taking verbal abuse from passersby for hours. I was practicing empathy when I said, "Hours of that would be extremely painful. If you'll allow me, I want to apologize for every disrespectful thing those people said." That expression of genuine understanding opened his heart wide for the miracle that followed.

You already know so much of what I just told you, don't you? You've been practicing the language of the heart since you first opened your eyes. For example, you already read cues about whether a person's heart is open. You sense a connection or its absence. You pick up on whether a person is focused or scattered, vulnerable or defensive. Body language signals mood and intent to you. If a person wants to talk, and if you're paying attention, you don't have to think about how messages are being sent—you just know.

As God's delivery agent, you simply get to be more intentional about what is already a second language to you.

Step 4

Deliver the Miracle

In this step in the process, we actively partner with the Spirit to deliver the miracle for God. Our role is to facilitate and invite, responding to the Spirit's guidance. That's why I say that even though the miracle itself is God's work, the step of delivering the miracle is our responsibility.

> _Even though the miracle itself is God's work, the step of delivering the miracle is our responsibility._

Until now in the delivery process, our role has been like John the Baptist's—preparing the way for God. Through circumstance and miracle-specific signals, we have been led to both the person and the need God has in mind. And we've done our part to open the person's heart.

Now it's God's turn to act. Thankfully, He desires to deliver miracles through us even more than we want Him to. That means we can relax. We don't have to try to understand exactly how our unseen partner works. We only have to trust that He _will_ and that we have a necessary role in the event. In this step of the process, God often guides us to do or say something important during the miracle delivery process that we wouldn't have thought of otherwise.

So there you are, God's delivery person, standing at the door of a person's life. The heart is open. What comes next?

Here is a sequence I find helpful:

Take your thoughts off yourself and place your faith consciously and directly in God's Spirit to lead. Continue making eye contact with, and focus completely on, the other person. What needs to happen next will depend on the kind of miracle that is in order. What does God want to happen? Does the person need to:

- receive something?
- let go of something?
- make a choice of the will?
- experience a breakthrough of insight about an important life issue?

Search for the emotional obstacle or limiting belief. Watch for the tender spot (the rise in emotional temperature) that indicates a need or injury. Often all it takes is the right question from you for the tender spot to suddenly appear.

Speak to the heart. God will guide you to say the right thing, so you don't need to get overly cautious or start second-guessing yourself. Jesus told His disciples not to be anxious ahead of time about what to say in a difficult situation when they were asked to speak for Him: "For the Holy Spirit will teach you in that very hour what you ought to say."[2]

You might find yourself quoting a Bible verse you didn't even know you'd memorized or suggesting a solution that hadn't been in your thoughts a second ago. Plenty of times you won't even realize what you said or why it mattered until later. Sometimes you won't notice, but the other person will—"I think God must have sent you!"

Give God time to act. You'll know when this is a good idea, because at the time you won't know what else to do! You need to get out of the way. God will begin to work in the heart in one way or another. Purposely slow down. Stop talking. Use more pauses. Consciously depend upon the Spirit, and pray silently.

I remember doing exactly that as I spoke with Owen that night. It was obvious that it would take a miracle to set Owen free. Keenly aware of my inadequacy, I'd raised all of my spiritual antennas to receive God's direction. What I sensed Him leading me to do was to be very straightforward and not worry about anyone else in the room. I was careful in leading Owen to realize the truth for himself: *If God clearly called me into ministry, He will clearly call me out of it.*

Keep in mind, God could have been calling Owen to quit, and He could have brought me to that room to help him do it. I didn't know. My goal was to help him find solid ground, then let God show us what to do from there.

As I challenged Owen about his decision process, I could tell that the Spirit was at work in his heart. I think everyone there that night could. It was visible in Owen's posture, in his pauses, on his face. And it was equally clear the moment the miracle was delivered. When Owen declared, "I won't quit," everyone in the room knew for sure that God had done a mighty work in Owen's heart.

At that moment his heart language revealed a new truth: He wasn't fighting anymore. He wasn't angry and despairing. He had fallen into God's arms in complete and peaceful surrender. We could see freedom and relief written all over his face.

I want to add a few more thoughts here about the role of prayer in a miracle delivery. You may have noticed that many stories reveal the delivery agent actively praying:

- Richard prayed with April about her baby's health.
- John prayed with Terrence in prison, asking God to reunite him with his daughter.
- Jessica asked her friends for urgent prayers for Leila, who—unbeknown to Jessica or her friends—was at that moment attempting to take her life.

In each case, the prayer became strategic for the miracle delivery. Yet none of these events unfolded in quite the same way: April received God's comfort and encouragement from a stranger in the middle of an airport. Terrence received an answer to his prayer in the form of his daughter's visit—a week and a half after John led him in prayer. (Did John still deliver a personal miracle? Absolutely!) And Jessica wasn't present with her friend Leila when God led her to pray or when God intervened to save Leila's life.

All of our delivery examples show that this part of the process can look different in different situations. One wonderful constant, though, is that the recipient is nearly always the first one to know that a miracle has taken place. Often he will say something that lets you know this is the case: "Wow, that was an amazing breakthrough for me!" Or "How did you know?" Or simply, "That was a miracle!"

Which leads to the last step in the process: making sure that the Person who did the miracle, not the delivery agent, gets properly recognized.

_____ Step 5 _____

Transfer the Credit

For delivery agents like you and me, our mission is not complete until we have shined the spotlight on what God has just accomplished. We intentionally do everything in our power to help the person make the all-important leap between the wonderful experience and the wonderful source of that experience—God Himself.

> *Our mission is not complete until we have shined the spotlight on what God has just accomplished.*

To give God credit means showing gratitude. But thankfulness is just the beginning. You might remember the story from the Gospels where Jesus healed ten lepers yet only one returned to give thanks. Notice how Luke records this man's response:

One of them, when he saw that he was healed, returned, and with a loud voice glorified God, and fell down on his face at His feet, giving Him thanks.[3]

Thankfulness to God focuses on how we feel about His gift, whereas glorifying God focuses on what we now know to be true about the Giver.

God is the ultimate source of the miracle. After a personal miracle, wor-shiping Him with gratitude, sincerity, thankfulness—and maybe even with a "loud voice"—is the ultimate acknowledgment that we really understand what just happened.

The closer we help the miracle recipient get to that kind of truthful response, the more completely we will have delivered the miracle.

You'll find that sometimes your encounters come to a close with a partial transfer (see how my conversation ended with the van driver, chapter 4). When you're dealing with people who don't seem to have an open relationship with God at the time, you need to bring their attention to a personal, caring God in a way that feels natural, not "churchy," to them.

Of course, sometimes a miracle unfolds in such a way that God's involve-ment is never in doubt. This is what makes prayer miracles such a great vehi-cle for revealing God's goodness and power. When God answers a specific request with a miracle, His hand is immediately evident.

Or take Owen's experience at the men's retreat. It happened in a setting where transferring credit to God came naturally. Every man present that night enthusiastically praised and worshiped God for His wonderful works.

How do we make sure God gets the credit?

I think the first thing is to help the other person put words to what just happened. Help him recognize that it was God who just showed up. But don't tell him that. If that's what obviously happened, help him reach the conclusion for himself. For example, you might begin by asking, "What just happened?" If God did something in his heart, he'll be quick to say some-thing like, "That was God!" or, "I can't believe what just happened—it feels miraculous!"

It's so important for people to hear themselves saying in their own words what happened. That way the meaning of the event—not just the event itself—rises into their awareness and stays in their memory.

As with opening the heart, the step of leading a person to understand what happened and to respond to God is our responsibility. It's our work—and wonderful privilege—to link that person's heart to God's actions so that he or she can express appreciation to God. I typically move through this in three stages.

First, I help the other person *identify and describe the specific need that was met.* For this I might use leading questions like these:

- "You don't feel that fear anymore, do you?"
- "Do you see the cost of bitterness differently now?"
- "Something just changed inside you, didn't it? What was it?"

Second, I help him *express how he feels about what God did.* For example, I might ask:

- "How do you feel about what God just did?"
- "What did God show you about how much He really cares about you?"

Finally, I help him *transfer the appropriate credit to God.* I might say something like this:

- "Can you say a short prayer to God, thanking Him for that gift? Or may I offer a prayer for you?"
- "Don't you think God would like to know how you're feeling about Him right now?"

For many, what they say next will be the first time in their lives they have expressed glory to God for something He did for them personally.

I hope you're seeing by now that transferring the credit might sound optional—like the bow on top of a nicely wrapped present—but it's not. It really goes to the heart of what we're talking about in *You Were Born for This.*

Good people doing good works in the world is not enough to fully accomplish what God wants done. God seeks to reveal Himself in majesty and truth in our generation—and to do so through us. That's why a miracle just delivered and received is a one-of-a-kind opportunity to give Him the glory He deserves.

When your miracle appointment has fully transferred the credit to God through a heartfelt statement or prayer, it's time to celebrate. You've just completed a miracle delivery!

Five words, another story to tell

You've seen a process described that God can use in your life. It begins when you get up in the morning as a person who has asked to be sent. Then it has you partnering with God for a personal miracle in an exciting sequence of events from "Hello" to "Mission accomplished."

When I teach seminars on this subject, people rehearse the sequence to one another: *Identify. Isolate. Open. Deliver. Transfer.*

Five words.

Five steps in the process.

Another miracle successfully delivered!

In the next section you're going to apply these five steps to three different kinds of personal miracles. In each of the three following chapters, I'll show you how to become increasingly skillful at partnering with God for miraculous results.

Part 4

THREE KEYS
TO SPECIAL DELIVERY
MIRACLES

Introduction to the Special Delivery Keys

In part 2 we explored the power of four big ideas we called Miracle Life Keys—the Master, People, Spirit, and Risk keys. Miracle Life Keys describe actions that consistently unlock and sustain our potential to partner with God for a life of miracles. These four keys are all about us—about an ongoing personal transaction between God and us.

Having learned the signals and steps involved in delivering personal miracles, we now turn our attention to the second set of keys. Each of these unlocks a miracle for a specific and universal human need. I call them Special Delivery Keys. These three keys are all about other people—about what God wants to do supernaturally through you to meet a specific need for them.

You've probably either sent or received a package marked "Special Delivery." The label means the delivery agent will handle the package with extra care to ensure it gets delivered in the right way to the right person. In a similar way, when Heaven sends an agent to deliver a special delivery miracle, a few extra guidelines apply. For example:

- A special delivery miracle usually begins and ends in the context of a conversation.
- The conversation surfaces universal cues indicating that God wants to meet a specific need in a specific way.
- The delivery agent applies biblical truths that reveal what must happen for the miracle to occur.
- The delivery agent follows in sequence the five steps to deliver the miracle.
- Because both the need and the outcome that God wants are known, the agent guides the conversation toward a predictable result.

The three needs we address—money, life dream, and forgiveness—not only are universal but also represent the kinds of personal miracles that seem to be needed the most. Further, they represent areas where most people suffer from misconceptions about the topic. Once we understand what the Bible teaches for each need, we can become intentional and increasingly skilled in delivering miracles to the people who need them.

Here's a preview:

The Money Key unlocks biblical insights that prepare you to deliver a miracle of financial provision to a person in need. The miracle happens because God sends you and His financial resources to connect with a person who has a specific financial need.

The Dream Key unlocks biblical insights that prepare you to deliver a breakthrough miracle to those who need to embrace and achieve their God-given life dream. When people who have misunderstood or discarded their life dream suddenly seize upon the truth and commit to pursuing it, their lives improve in dramatic ways.

The Forgiveness Key unlocks biblical insights that empower you to partner with the Spirit for miracle breakthroughs in the areas connected to wounds of the heart. When you identify the wrong beliefs that keep a person suffering from unforgiveness and also the right beliefs necessary to bring healing, God works through you to deliver a wonderful miracle of forgiveness and freedom.

Of course, these aren't the only areas where God wants to meet needs. But you'll find, as I have, that hardly a day passes when you don't meet people who are burdened by a financial need, confused about their purpose in life, or stuck in bitterness and resentment.

One of the best things about these miracles is that we don't have to wonder what God wants to happen. When He directs us to someone with one of these needs, we approach the person with confidence. We know that God wants the need met, we know the truth that brings life change, and we know how to partner with Him to deliver the miracle. That's why we call these the keys to special delivery miracles.

The three needs we address not only are universal but also represent the kinds of personal miracles that seem to be needed the most.

10

The Money Key

*You were born to deliver miracles
of financial provision*

One late night after a speaking engagement in Johannesburg, my son, David, and I were suddenly attacked by the same desperate thought: we just had to have some ice cream. It's true. My son and I seem to share the double-strength dessert gene. We rushed back to the hotel where we were staying in hopes that the restaurant would still be open. We made it just in time.

When the waitress came to take our order, I said, "You have no idea how glad we are to find you! We've rushed back here from across town just for ice cream."

What she said next was heartbreaking. "I'm so sorry, sir. We just closed for the night. I can't serve you ice cream, but could I get you some coffee?"

David and I looked at each other. Had we hurried to the restaurant for nothing? I decided to ask again. "Sure, we'll take some decaf. But is there any way you could find some ice cream for two guys who would really appreciate it?"

She smiled. "I'll see what I can do."

As she walked away, I received an unexpected but unmistakable God nudge. In some way we were here for her too, not just for ice cream. The nudge was clear and specific: *Give her a big tip*. Actually, it was more like *Give her a very big tip*.

And we hadn't gotten any ice cream yet.

After I told David about the nudge, he said, "Dad, I was just thinking the same thing. A really big tip for what, though?"

We both laughed. But my laughter concealed the discomfort I was feeling. You see, I'd been to the bank recently and happened to have a large roll of rand (the South African currency) in my pocket. In my heart God had clearly linked the very big tip with that roll of bills. They seemed to be one and the same.

Well, I can tell you that God loves people who love ice cream. The waitress came back from the kitchen with two big bowls of it...and coffees to go with it.

As we were finishing, I took the bills out of my pocket, folded them into a bundle, and held it ready under the table. When the waitress walked up with the check, I said, "You were so kind to find us that ice cream when the kitchen was closed. We appreciate your extraordinary service and want to give you a tip that reflects that." Then I slipped the money into her apron pocket. I didn't even want David to see how much it was.

Can you guess what I was feeling at that moment? Not heroic, insightful, or generous. No, more like awkward. I didn't want to be misinterpreted. In a hotel in Johannesburg, like in many other places, the only reason a man would give that kind of money to a woman is if he's trying to buy her favors for the night. What was God up to?

Three minutes later the waitress came rushing back to our table. "You know Jesus, don't you?" she said, tears in her eyes.

"Yes."

"I knew it! This is a miracle!" she exclaimed. "I have a baby, and we couldn't pay rent, and the landlord was going to kick us out of our apartment tomorrow morning. I prayed to God on the way to work just this afternoon, 'Please, God, send us the money, or we'll be living on the street.'"

She wiped at her eyes. "Sir, this amount is exactly the rent I owe—*to the rand*. That's how I knew you know Jesus."

David and I walked out of that restaurant two happy men.

Ready and willing

Do you see the signs of God at work in our ice cream adventure? We certainly did! To me it highlights several key elements of the miracle deliveries we've talked about:

- God is at work behind the scenes, orchestrating the place and timing for a miracle connection.
- God nudges a sent one to connect with a person in need.
- God arranges the event so that when the delivery happens, the recipient knows in her heart that God intervened specifically for her.

But that night God was creative. He nudged me to do something that felt excessive and foolish. I knew whom I was supposed to give the money to, but I had no idea why or how much she needed. While I could have bumped her to isolate the need, I didn't. Honestly, it didn't even occur to me. And I think I know why.

God wanted to demonstrate His abundant goodness in a most remarkable fashion. So He decided to use a couple of ice cream fanatics to bring an anxious mom a supernatural experience of His loving care in a way she would never forget.

How you and I think about and manage our money matters greatly to God. Jesus spoke of money often, and He spent most of His time with those who didn't have much. He fed the hungry, helped his friends deal with taxes,

God intends for us to use our money to display His goodness and faithfulness in miraculous ways.

honored those who gave out of their poverty. Clearly, God wants us to be both thoughtful and generous with our resources.

But if we stop there, we miss a much bigger idea—that God intends for us to use our money to display His goodness and faithfulness in miraculous ways.

The first special delivery miracle I want to talk about has to do with this area of universal interest and need: financial provision. Can you think of a greater concern for people all over the world today? How would your life change if God worked through you on a regular basis to miraculously meet the money-related needs of others?

The Money Key unlocks a miracle of financial provision for another person. The miracle happens because God sends you with His resources to a person who has a need. Your miracle delivery is based on powerful Bible truths about how God works supernaturally through people on earth to meet a financial need.

Like the two other miracles we'll explore in this section, the money miracle is unusually predictable. By that I mean, from the beginning of your miracle appointment, you know exactly why Heaven has brought you together, and you know that God seeks to meet a financial need through you.

Even though we commonly feel protective and even possessive of our resources, the promise of the Money Key is liberating and rewarding. You'll discover that the reward of partnering with God in practical, visible ways becomes an event you genuinely look forward to.

Financial miracles often begin with a nudge from God. That nudge is likely to take you by surprise. (Consider His plans for my roll of South

African rand.) But they all have the same goal: a miracle that switches all the spotlights on God the Giver and causes someone to exclaim, "Wow! God sent you to meet my financial need!"

The Money Key miracle is rooted in a faith-filled application of Paul's advice in 1 Timothy 6, where he writes:

> *Let them do good, that they be rich in good works, ready to give, willing to share.*[1]

Notice especially the phrases "ready to give, willing to share." These words lay the foundation for miracle missions to meet the financial needs of others. We prepare ourselves to partner with God in a money miracle by applying these twin directives—willingness and readiness—to the way we approach our financial priorities. Our precommitment alerts Heaven that we are fully prepared to act when God brings a miracle opportunity our way.

In case you were thrown off by the big roll of bills in my story, let me reassure you that God does miracles just as easily with a five or ten as with a hundred-dollar note. But we won't get anywhere unless we understand God's agenda for money and how He actually gets a financial provision to a person in need.

How God transfers money

How, exactly, does God move money around to meet needs on earth? Specifically, how would He do that for you?

Could Heaven somehow transfer cash into your account?

Could Heaven print some currency and drop it out of the sky onto your doorstep?

Could God, who owns the cattle on a thousand hills, as Psalm 50 puts it, take out a loan on His earthly assets to meet your need?

Could an angel deliver the money from the vaults of Heaven?

When it comes to prayers for a financial miracle, Heaven depends on people for answers.

The answer may shock you. While He could do all those things, every indication is that He doesn't. God only gets funds to a person in need when another human being releases some of his or her funds for that purpose. When it comes to prayers for a financial miracle, Heaven depends on people for answers.

A verse in the Bible succinctly describes God's transfer process:

Whoever is generous to the poor lends to the LORD.[2]

Surprising, isn't it? And the verse doesn't say it is *like* a loan—it *is* a loan. The moment a generous person gives in response to a God nudge, a second, invisible transfer takes place in Heaven. With those same funds, the generous person "lends to the LORD." And now God has funds to answer the person's prayer with a financial miracle.

Now look at the universal principle revealed in the second part of the verse:

And He [God] will pay back what he has given.[3]

Do you see it? Yet another surprise is linked to the first: a loan to God for His work will be paid back by Heaven. Jesus confirmed this principle of divine repayment many times. In fact, He said that even a cup of water will be credited to the giver.[4]

After understanding how this process occurs, you can understand why God loves to initiate miracles with money. Let's revisit the sequence of a financial miracle from human need to supernatural provision:

- A person has a real financial need.

- Heaven either hears his prayers for help or recognizes his unstated needs.
- Heaven decides to answer the financial need with a specific amount and identifies an optimum situation and time for delivery.
- Heaven nudges a person who has the funds and opportunity to meet those needs.
- The delivery person gives the money to the one in need, preparing the way for the Lord to receive full credit and appreciation.

When you consider how many people need a financial miracle and how few people respond to a God nudge that's related to finances, you begin to see why so many opportunities await anyone who wants to partner with God for a financial miracle.

If that's you, where could you start today? Let me show you.

I want to introduce you to one of my favorite practical tools for inviting financial miracles. One thing that makes it so powerful—and enjoyable—is that you're giving money that isn't yours.

I call it the God Pocket.

What is a God Pocket?

The God Pocket is a specific location in your wallet or purse where you keep money you have devoted to God so you can give it to someone in need as soon as He nudges you to do so. In the same way the Elisha bump—"How can I help you?"—launches you into an exciting life of servant miracles, the God Pocket launches you into an exciting life of financial miracles.

The idea for the God Pocket was born out of the frustration that my wife, Darlene, and I felt about our giving early in our marriage. It's not that we weren't generous to our church and other worthy causes. We were. Yet when we gave to individuals, God didn't seem to show up very often in the process. The more we thought about Paul's advice to be "ready to give, willing to share," the more we realized that our problem might lie not in *what* or *where* we gave but in *how* we gave.

What would happen if we were "ready to give" *in advance* so we could respond tangibly and without hesitation to a nudge from God? The simple tool of the God Pocket became our answer.

To prepare for a God Pocket miracle, take these five helpful steps:

First, decide how much money you are going to put into your God Pocket. These funds aren't the ones you give to your church or other organizations but are additional and are specifically for God to use in delivering a financial miracle to others. If you're confused about how much to start with, ask God to help. He blesses most when you joyfully give a sum that is meaningful to you.[5]

> *To devote something, in the biblical sense, means you are dedicating it in advance to God.*

Second, devote that amount of money directly to God. To devote something, in the biblical sense, means you are dedicating it in advance to another person—in this case, to God. When you devote, say, your twenty dollars to God, you are expressing to Him, "From this point forward, this twenty dollars is Yours. I will carry it in Your name until You show me who it is for."

Third, deposit your devoted money into your God Pocket. Choose a special spot in your wallet or purse where you won't get it confused with your other funds. The only money that goes into the God Pocket is money you have set apart in advance as belonging to God, not you. From now on, you keep only devoted money there. It is God's Pocket.

Fourth, determine right then that when God nudges, you won't debate with Him or talk yourself out of the assignment. Remember, you're not responding to apparent needs but to a God nudge. You are trusting God to meet a need He knows about and specifically reveals to you.

A good friend of our family's, Nancy, felt nudged to deliver her God Pocket money to a woman she didn't know well. But when Nancy drove up to the woman's house, she saw that it was nicer than her own. At that moment, Nancy told me, she felt strongly tempted to turn around. But she didn't. Once inside, she discovered that the recipient was in dire financial straits. For the woman in need, the God Pocket was an unmistakable miracle of provision.

Fifth, consciously depend upon the Lord to nudge you when, where, and to whom He wants His funds delivered. He will! You don't have to fret about who He has in mind or when He'll make His move. He might nudge you today or this week or next month. Meantime, you are free to go about your business as a sent person—"ready to give, willing to share."

What makes such simple preparations for a financial miracle so effective? Think about how many times you have been nudged by God, but in your confusion about what it meant or what to do, you talked yourself out of doing anything. The God Pocket changes that. If you're carrying money that is no longer yours—money that you've emotionally detached from— you're free to act when God nudges. And when you do, you'll do so with freedom, joy, and expectation.

Be careful to treat your God Pocket money with utmost respect. For example, just because you're carrying it around doesn't mean it's a slush fund you can borrow from when a need arises or when you're looking at a sale item you just can't pass up. It's not even money you'll put in the offering plate at church. Remember? The money in your God Pocket already belongs to God. So until He nudges you toward a particular person, don't touch it.

Sometimes the need God wants to meet is not only monetary but also deeply emotional. Through my God Pocket experiences, He has memorably demonstrated what He meant when He described Himself as "merciful and gracious, longsuffering, and abounding in goodness."[6]

And what exactly does "abounding in goodness" look like? Well, different in different situations. Here's what it looked like in a department store in the Rocky Mountains.

"Somebody sent me"

On a trip out west, I needed a wristwatch in a hurry. (I've discovered that a visiting speaker who doesn't watch the time rarely gets invited back.) Standing at a counter in a department store, I was about to make my choice when I couldn't help noticing a shopper farther down the counter. She had been staring at a particular watch for some time, apparently trying to talk herself into buying it.

"That is a beautiful watch," I said. "It looks like it was made for you!" The turquoise trim on the watch matched her Native American attire perfectly.

"You really think so?" she replied.

"I do. Why don't you get it?"

She said, "Oh, I could never afford this watch."

"That's too bad," I said. "You might not find a watch quite like that one again."

She said, "I know," but gently set the watch back down on the counter. I was ready to try on the watch I had selected for myself when I received an unexpected but distinct God nudge. *Oh,* I thought to myself. *Her.* I was taken by surprise. *A turquoise watch? Right now?* But the signals were unmistakable.

I caught her eye. "Um, it's not hard to see you would really love this watch. May I have the privilege of buying that watch for you?"

"What?"

"Wouldn't you like the watch?"

"Yes, very much. But you can't buy it for me!"

"No, I can't," I said, hesitating. How do you explain your God Pocket to a stranger? You can't really. But you can talk about the real owner of those funds.

"A special friend of mine instructed me to carry around some of His funds," I continued. "He asked me to keep my eye out for a person whom I think He would really want to help with His money. When I find that person, I'm supposed to use it. My friend would definitely want you to have this watch."

"Really?" she said, trying to process what I had just said.

"Oh yes. It's true. He'd really enjoy buying it for you." I motioned to the salesclerk for assistance.

"Oh my goodness!" she said. She stared at the watch, then at me. Then she said, almost to herself, "I had lost all confidence in mankind."

That's when I really noticed her face for the first time. It was heavily lined and bore an expression of deep sadness.

I said, "You have really been hurt, haven't you? You've been wounded many times."

"Yes, I have." Her eyes were tearing up.

"Well, Somebody who knew about your wounds sent me all the way from Atlanta because He wants you to know that He deeply cares about you. Might you know who that is?"

A light seemed to click on for her. "It's God, isn't it?"

"He does love you, doesn't He?" I said quietly.

She was brushing away tears as I made the purchase with my God Pocket funds and handed the watch to her.

But God wasn't finished. "Jesus knew sorrow more than anyone you'll ever meet. Every time you look at this watch, remember that God loves you and wants your heart not only to be healed but to sing!"

As I walked out of that store, my heart was singing too.

The five steps of delivery for a financial miracle

You might have recognized a familiar delivery pattern—or at least recurring parts of it—in the stories in this chapter. That's because how you deliver a financial miracle follows a similar pattern to the other miracles we talk about in this book. The five-step process I'll apply next will help you intentionally partner with God to deliver a financial miracle.

Step 1: Identify the person God wants to help. With money miracles God leads us with a nudge. Take what happened when David and I were waiting for ice cream in Johannesburg: God nudged me clearly about the waitress. To overcome my uncertainties and fears, I had to purposefully exercise my faith and move forward, trusting the Lord to guide as He promised.

With the woman at the watch counter, God also initiated the process with a nudge. With a money miracle, that sequence seems to happen a lot; we are directed *toward* a person (the nudge), then often we recognize what we are to give the person during the process.

Especially in this area of finances, where we often encounter people in financial stress, we must remember that not every need is an invitation from God to use our God Pocket. Besides, external appearances are often unreliable, as our friend Nancy found out. Only God knows all the facts about someone's actual financial needs. That's why we must give His nudges higher priority than our own feelings or observations. That includes the cues we see.

The God Pocket is directly related to the God nudge, not a cue or bump. In other words, the cue doesn't initiate the God Pocket; only the nudge does that. Why? Because our heart may go out to the needs of another, but that doesn't give us the right to make decisions about where and when and to whom God wants to distribute His funds. Of course, we always have the freedom to give our own funds to someone in need, just not from the designated funds in the God Pocket.

The cue may be an invitation for us to use our funds to help someone, but unless Heaven agrees with a nudge or some type of confirmation, then we must not make those decisions for God. Furthermore, we have a fixed amount of funds that are available for the God Pocket, and we don't know if God may want us to give His funds to someone else two hours later. If we empty His account for Him, we are assuming authority we don't have. The banker doesn't spend the depositor's money for him!

Step 2: Isolate the need. Once God has used a nudge to bring you to the person He has in mind for you to help, you may find yourself needing to use a cue or a bump to identify the particular need God wants to meet.

Recently I had a parking lot conversation with Charles, a hardworking man who appeared to have more than one significant need. He talked mostly about the struggles he was having with his teenagers and at work. But when he made a passing comment about his need to fix his front teeth, his expression changed. He became quiet.

"Do you have a dentist?" I asked.

"Sure," he said. "No insurance, though. And where our finances are at, my teeth won't ever get to the top of the list."

Suddenly I sensed why God had put me into this conversation. Among all the needs Charles faced, his obvious need for dental work seemed to cause him the most personal pain.

Step 3: Open the heart and increase the desire. With Charles, I sensed that the need I'd been brought to address was clear. I could tell by his tone of voice, facial expression, and body language that his heart was already opening.

An additional step I often take at this point is to help the person clarify and increase his desire for the specific miracle that God brought me to deliver. To accomplish this, I try to focus the person's attention on the single, isolated need, brushing away all other competing desires that might surface. Why is this so important? I want to guide the person to the firm conclusion that he or she indeed will use these funds for the identified purpose and not misuse the funds when I'm no longer present.

Another reason to clarify and increase the recipient's desire is that, at the moment the miracle is delivered, I want the person to have the strongest possible emotional response of thanksgiving to God. The more powerful the emotional response, the more credit and glory God receives and the more lasting the memory of His goodness will be in the recipient's heart.

That's why part of our role as a delivery person is to stir the desire of those who will receive the miracles. A simple question or two helps to get them more in touch with their deepest desires. Questions like "Why is that important to you?" or "If Heaven somehow granted that to you, how would you feel?" We are simply focusing their attention on the feelings of hope, pain, or despair that are tightly wrapped around the need.

I asked Charles, "If funds were available to get your teeth fixed or to be used for something else, what would you do?" I was asking him to put the degree of his desire into words.

Charles shook his head in disbelief. "Well, that's not going to happen." His voice got quiet and dreamy. "But if it did…I believe I'd be a new man. I wouldn't feel embarrassed all the time."

Clearly, the personal anguish caused by his dental problem was number one on his list, and the degree of his desire was intense.

"Well, Charles, I have some wonderful news I would like to share with you," I began. It was time for Step 4.

Step 4: Deliver the miracle. Perhaps by now you know what I said to Charles next: "A while back someone entrusted me with some money. This person told me that when I saw a need He'd want to meet if He were here, I should pass His money on for Him." As often happens, Charles's surprise and joy immediately demonstrated that he understood who was behind that miracle.

When you are delivering the funds, continue speaking to the other person's heart, relating directly to his need. Focus on his emotional response. Remember, the Holy Spirit is at work in his heart to draw him closer to God through this miracle. And a personal, powerful revelation of God's compassion is a very important outcome of any miracle we deliver for Him.

When we deliver the Lord's funds with excellence, the person's heart will open wide toward God. You've experienced this in your own life—God came through for you in such a way that you spontaneously poured out to Him your intense joy, thanksgiving, and praise. Heaven loves that kind of response!

Of course, the financial miracle started with God. But you asked to be sent, you asked for God's heart for the ones you will be sent to, and you invited His Spirit to do God's supernatural work through you. So when He leads you with nudges and prompts, you can be sure that He is actively at work in you and in the other person as you move forward in faith. Proactively and confidently depend on Him to guide you and to communicate His thoughts through you.

Step 5: Transfer the credit. You're trying to do God's work in such a way that He gets all the credit. God is the one who brought you and the other person together so His resource could be delivered. You just provided the hand-off.

Think of yourself as Heaven's bank teller, facilitating a heavenly withdrawal at the Owner's request.

Sometimes God's glory shines forth so obviously that everyone can see it. The waitress in Johannesburg happened to be a follower of Jesus Christ. And she was in such desperate straits that she prayed on the way to work for a miracle of provision. When she discovered what I had slipped into her apron pocket, she knew instantly—without any communication from me—that God had answered her prayer. Her praise and thanks flew immediately to Him, not me.

But if the recipient starts going on about what a nice person you are, it's time to help her get the picture back in focus. "Remember, this is not my money" is an important sentence. Another helpful statement is "The owner instructed me to carry it around until I saw someone who needed it."

Then gently lead the recipient toward her own conclusion about the source of the gift. To the woman at the watch counter, I said, "Somebody who knew about your wounds sent me all the way from Atlanta because He wants you to know that He deeply cares about you. Might you know who that is?" By then she knew who I meant, and that gave me a chance to tell her that God loved her.

You'll know you've hit a grand slam when the person is so absorbed with the fact that God has showed up dramatically to meet her need and show His love that she forgets you're there!

Common questions, helpful answers

Over the years I've heard several questions from people who want to serve God with their money but hesitate for understandable reasons. Here are a few of the most common concerns.

Aren't we supposed to give money in secret, not in public as with the God Pocket? I applaud people who are honestly trying to live by Jesus' words in Matthew 6:1–4 about giving in secret. But this advice was aimed at people who were selfishly motivated to get the most public recognition possible for their giving. Jesus was confronting the prideful model offered by the religious sect known as the Pharisees, who were deliberately ostentatious in their giving.

But with the Money Key, we're being deliberate about something else entirely: bringing maximum credit to God. Inviting Him to reveal Himself through money always means deflecting attention away from oneself and toward God.

It's *God's* pocket, *God's* money, and *God's* miracle, after all. Our work for Him is successful only if people recognize what happened, not as a good work on our part, but as visible proof that God did something wonderful and we were merely His delivery agent.

In the Sermon on the Mount, Jesus commanded this direct approach: "Let your light so shine before men, that they may see your good works and glorify your Father in Heaven."[7] Jesus' command reminds us that we can give so creatively and purposefully that one outcome is assured: God receives great glory.

What if I choose to give the money to the wrong person? This could happen if you act without a nudge or misinterpret a nudge. God is so eager to give financial miracles to people who need them that He's going to clearly and unmistakably reveal to you the person He has in mind for you. In my experience, when a person first steps out to serve God with money, He leads with baby steps. With practice, our ability to sense His leading improves.

What if the person uses the money for wrong things, like drugs? This can happen, but in my experience it's much rarer than you might fear. Remember that a financial miracle is tailor-made by God to meet a specific need in a person's life. Ultimately, we trust that He will guide us to the right people and to the specific need He wants to meet. Of course, we also need to be wise and learn from our mistakes. I've made a few, but thankfully God can use a gift that might seem misdirected at the time to make an impact later.

Taking God's gifts to extremes

While you and I are understandably cautious about giving away our resources when we see no apparent benefit or payback to us, Jesus isn't. Have you ever noticed? Consider His advice on how to serve up dinner:

> *When you give a banquet, invite the poor, the crippled, the lame, the blind, and you will be blessed. Although they cannot repay you, you will be repaid.*[8]

Jesus is telling us something breathtaking—and utterly life changing—about Heaven's view of giving. I would paraphrase it like this: now that you've signed up for a miracle life, don't play it safe. Give to those most overlooked or rejected by others. Give them a feast they'll never forget. By all means, risk getting nothing back, because now you know the truth: God repays those who lend to Him.[9]

By all means, risk getting nothing back, because now you know the truth: God repays those who lend to Him.

Sounds extreme, doesn't it? But by now you should understand the powerful *why* of going to extremes—it's exactly this kind of giving that invites God Himself to become visible, to blaze in glory for an unforgettable moment in a person's life.

How could you throw a feast for someone in need today? Where would you start?

You could start by preparing in advance to give with a God Pocket. He has so many miracles waiting to be delivered through you. And you were born to reveal His extravagant goodness and generosity.

———◆———

11

The Dream Key

You were born to deliver miracles of life purpose

Walking up to the lectern, I thought, *Well, this is a first.* The Mary Hall Freedom House on Atlanta's north side is a residential program for women from the streets who are alcoholics or addicts or both. For some reason, in a lifetime of speaking and teaching around the world, I'd never faced quite this kind of audience. But my main concern wasn't the audience. It was my topic. I was here to teach about big life dreams.

"Bruce, are you sure that's the best topic for that crowd?" a friend had asked before I went. "It almost feels mean to talk about big dreams to people who are in such a hard place."

If you ever want to clear your head about what really matters in life, spend a day at a rehab center. You'll come away inspired, humbled, grateful. Each one of the 150 women I met at Mary Hall proved to be a walking testament to courage in the face of cruel odds. A woman named Joyce, who said drugs had ruined the past fifteen years of her life, put things in black and white: "I knew my life would end if I didn't change."

But big dreams? These are women who just want to stay clean and sober for another day. Who long for the day when they can be reunited with their children. Who hope for the day when their boyfriend will stop beating them. Who dream about a safe place they could call home. Not one of them appears to be on the fast track to anything you or I would think of as a desirable life.

So why did I feel God leading me so strongly to talk to them about seizing their dream? It didn't take long to find out.

"I believe that you and I were created by God to pursue a big life dream," I announced. "Usually it's something we've been aware of most of our lives. It's not something we make up. It's just there."

Then I got straight to the point. "How many of you would say that you have a life dream? Maybe it's been forgotten, maybe it's been locked away, but you'd say to me, 'Bruce, I've *always* had a big dream of what I wanted to do with my life.'"

Hands shot up all over the room.

Think about this. Mary Hall Freedom House is a halfway house for folks trying to get from nowhere to anywhere else. And still, at least half the women knew they had a big life dream!

I've seen the same response all over the world. Ask children in villages or cities, slums or high-rises, and they'll tell you they already know what they want to be when they grow up. They can already feel it and taste it—they're already there. Then ask adults around the world if they still carry a big dream in their heart, and most will say, "I think so...somewhere in there...yes."

Over the next few hours with those brave women, I laid out what the Bible teaches about what we might call the DNA of our personal life purpose. I showed them why they should never stop believing in their dream, how to reclaim it if it had gotten lost along the way, and how to discover what the next step should be in their pursuit of it.

"Your big dream isn't just about you, you know," I said. "Your dream is a one-of-a-kind part of God's larger Dream for the world. Maybe that's why He cares about your dream even more than you do. He made you not just to have your own big dream but to overcome all the obstacles in your way and actually live it."

And it's never too late to start. Or start again.

As I talked to the women, I saw tears of pain and regret at opportunities lost. But I also saw hope returning. Some who had thought a big dream was not for them understood for the first time that everyone has one—that a woman in a halfway house who has never believed in, much less pursued, a big dream has one too. For others, God was opening the secret rooms of their heart where they'd long ago hidden away what they knew they were born to do. They began talking excitedly about passion and purpose—a life that promised more than just surviving another day.

By the end of the day, tears had turned to laughter as the women worked together to identify the next important, doable step they could take to set out again on their dream journey. I was honored just to be a witness.

Have you ever watched someone wake up to the promise of his life? Have you seen a man, burdened by years of hard work and responsibility, rediscover the wonder and incredible significance of his personal passion? It's like seeing the desert bloom after rain into a riot of color.

That thrill can be your part in an unforgettable miracle, and it's what I want to prepare you for in the pages ahead.

A big dream is the bull's-eye

What do I mean when I say big dream? Obviously, we all have numerous dreams over the course of our lives—dreams for our marriage, our children, our finances, and more. But when I say big dream, I'm referring to the driving desire to do something special, something that God put in your heart when He created you. He put it there for a very important reason. Follow your big dream, and you will pursue with passion the very thing He created you to do over the course of your whole life!

Let me ask, what percentage of the people you know would you say are actually living their big dream? Ten percent? Fifty percent? Ninety percent? Most groups I talk to, professional counselors included, place the number at the very low end of the scale.

If that's true—and I believe it is—then the cost in personal and cultural suffering would have to be staggering. Wouldn't it help explain why so many people today feel trapped in unhappiness, depression, addiction, anger, or apathy?

A person who is pursuing his dream is energized by hope and purpose. His path may not be smooth, but he has direction. Even the challenges reveal a larger meaning to him. Why? The big picture of his life—his reason for being here—is clear.

Compare that to the person who thinks his life has no higher purpose, no big idea or goal. Over time his enthusiasm will fade. He'll lose his way. Without knowing quite why, he'll feel forgotten by God. To fill the emptiness inside, he'll tend to give in to excuses, passivity, or choices that harm himself or others.

Do you recognize yourself or anyone you know in these patterns?

> *Ultimately, we are happiest when we are doing what God created us to do. And He created us to do His work by His power.*

Ultimately, we are happiest when we are doing what God created us to do. And He created us to do His work by His power. Living our big dream is the bull's-eye, the very center, of how we experience joy and purpose and how we contribute most to our world. The incredible promise of pursuing our big dream, along with the very real cost of not pursuing it, brings us to the Dream Key.

The Dream Key unlocks a miracle of life

purpose for others. God divinely connects you—a dream champion— with someone who is stuck or needs to know and fully embrace his God-created life dream. You deliver a miracle when God works through you supernaturally to help him take a crucial next step in his dream journey.

Sent ones (the Master Key) who have God's heart for others (the People Key), who know how to partner with God's Spirit for a miracle (the Spirit Key), and who exercise their faith (the Risk Key) can champion the big dream in another person's heart. And because a person's big dream is so important to God, we can rely on Him to intervene in miraculous ways as we help others discover and pursue their dream.

Like the other two keys described in this section—the Money and Forgiveness keys—the Dream Key leads to a special delivery miracle. By that I mean we follow a special set of delivery instructions. For example:

- We apply a set of biblical truths and practical steps that we know must be embraced for a miracle to occur.
- We follow the five steps of the delivery process.
- We guide the conversation toward a predictable outcome.

The opportunity for us as delivery agents is truly motivating. We know beyond a doubt what outcome God wants! That means, once we understand our part in the miracle, we can proceed with confidence and focused purpose to lead the other person to the miracle breakthrough he needs.

Whereas a money miracle is a provision miracle, I describe the dream miracle as a breakthrough miracle. When people who have misunderstood or discarded their dream suddenly seize upon the truth, their lives change in fundamental ways. Instead of confusion, they have clarity. Instead of apathy, motivation. Instead of being stuck, their lives show strong forward motion.

Invariably, they'll look back on their *aha!* moment with you as an unforgettable gift straight from God.

Helping others find or reignite their life dream might be something you already do with family or friends. You notice someone is struggling in this area, so you step in to guide and encourage. But as you'll soon discover, the Dream Key provides the understanding and the skills to be intentional with anyone you meet. It helps you be proactive about inviting God's Spirit to step in so that a breakthrough miracle occurs.

As you read this chapter, you may find yourself thinking about your own dream a lot—and that's what you should do! After all, you can't give away something you don't possess. Fully embracing your own life dream will bring you the fulfillment and sense of purpose God intends for you and, at the same time, will empower and motivate you to champion the big life dreams of others.

The gap in God's big dream

Maybe you noticed that with the People Key I didn't have to convince you that people need help. Or with the Money Key, that so many face financial shortfalls. But with this key, I want to show you a cluster of related truths about our purpose in life that get overlooked by millions. When that happens, they don't just miss out on the big dream they were born to pursue; they stop believing they ever had one.

Look with me now behind the veil of Heaven to discover two of those truths: why everyone has a big dream, and where everyone's dream comes from. As we've seen in previous chapters, the more we understand and embrace how Heaven works, the better we become at delivering miracles for God.

In Jeremiah 1 we can listen in as God explains to His servant how he was created to be a prophet:

> The word of the LORD came to me, saying:
>   "Before I formed you in the womb I knew you;
>   Before you were born I sanctified you;
>   I ordained you a prophet to the nations." [1]

Notice the sequence of events in this intriguing sentence: "Before I formed you in the womb I knew you." What happened first? First, God knew whom He wanted Jeremiah to be—in his case, "a prophet to the nations." Then God formed him in his mother's womb, giving him a unique set of strengths and weaknesses to match the significant calling of his life. In other words, before Jeremiah was formed in his mother's womb, God imagined and designed him for a special purpose. First came the purpose, then the person.

That's how two doctoral students created a new way to get information. Larry Page and Sergey Brin started with a purpose: find a better way to organize the world's information and make it accessible and useful. From there they came up with a new method for finding and ranking search results on the Web.

Only then did they create Google, now the world's best-known search engine.

God reveals to Jeremiah that He created him in a similar way. God had something He needed to get done. (You could say He had the job description before He had the job candidate.) At a particular point in history, God knew He would need a prophet exactly like Jeremiah. Why? A prophet exactly like Jeremiah would be custom-made to accomplish an important part of God's agenda for that exact time and place in human history.

Imagine a line from one side of this page to the other, with a tiny section missing in the middle. Like this:

_____[ ]_____

The line represents time from eternity past to eternity future; the tiny gap represents Jeremiah's life. Suppose the whole line represents God's story. God needed Jeremiah to be a prophet at a particular time and place so His larger story would be complete.

Did God do the same thing when He invented you and me? Yes, He did. For each of us, God starts with one thing He needs done and then creates us with both the desire and the potential to accomplish it.

How many people does God make to accomplish that one thing? Only one. You and I have been created and put on earth now to complete our part of God's big Dream. That means, by the way, that everything about us is a gift from God—our unique strengths *and* our glaring weaknesses. *Who* He made us to be fits *what* we're meant to do with our lives…perfectly!

The psalmist beautifully describes God's purpose-directed creative process for each of us:

> *When I was made in secret*
> *And skillfully wrought…*
> *Your eyes saw my substance, being yet unformed.*
> *And in Your book they all were written,*
> *The days fashioned for me,*
> *When as yet there were none of them.*[2]

These aren't just inspiring thoughts; they are life-changing truths. They declare something vital and opposite from what our culture declares. Consider:

- The world says you were born *without* a special purpose designed into your being. Therefore, you have to invent your dream if you want your life to have meaning.
- But the Bible reveals that your dream precedes you. God starts with His dream for you, and then He uniquely and lovingly forms you to desire the dream and to accomplish it for His glory.

Talk about a radical difference! That's why I can tell you that if a person sets out to pursue a life dream with doubts about its true origin, he's likely to end up cynical, sidetracked, and stuck. If he thinks that he (not God) invented his dream, why wouldn't he treat it as one goal that's no more important than some other goal? Under stress he'll be tempted to trade it away for something more convenient but much less fulfilling.

Our dream is why God formed us. It explains who we are and why we're here.

From one dreamer to another, I urge you to lay hold of these simple but amazing truths about the origin and importance of everyone's life dream:

- Our dream is invented by God, not us.
- Our dream is why God formed us. It explains who we are (and who we're not) and why we're here.
- Our dream was never meant to be optional. It is an indispensable part of God's Dream for this time and place.
- Our dream was never meant to be just a remote possibility for us but a completed achievement. God plans for each of us to accomplish our dream.

With these new paradigms in mind, we can become intentional about inviting a dream miracle with the people we meet, knowing that we are sent by God with this incredibly liberating and motivating message: *You were born to pursue and fulfill God's big dream for your life!*

We can ask God to lead us to people who don't know that or who have lost faith in God's dream for them. We can invite His Spirit to open eyes, make connections, and renew hidden hopes as we deliver a miracle breakthrough in life purpose.

"All I ever wanted"

Now you're ready to look again at a foundational scripture we cited in chapter 2:

We are his workmanship, created in Christ Jesus for good works, which God prepared beforehand that we should walk in them.[3]

We saw then that partnering intentionally with God on His miracle agenda for us is an important part of the good works we were created to do. As you might suspect, there is a direct relationship between the specific miracles God wants us to deliver and the big dream God has placed in our hearts.

Our dream—and all the passion, energy, and skills that go with it—is the powerful force or engine that propels us toward the good works that God has prepared ahead of time for us to do.

What happens if we never unleash that powerful force? never even realize it's there? Well, not only do we lose out in terms of personal fulfillment and significance, but critical tasks are left undone. A piece of God's big dream remains blank. Individuals, families, and communities can suffer tragic consequences.

That's what almost happened to Zack. From childhood he wanted to be in the marines. He used to turn his family's backyard into an imaginary battlefield where he could practice tactics and strategy. When he got to college, he enrolled in an officer training program, where he excelled. He couldn't wait to get in uniform and be a leader of men in combat. And anyone who knew Zack thought he was perfectly suited for the task.

There was one problem—Zack has a slight but unusual visual impairment. When he went to sign up, he learned that his condition would limit his options in a military career. That seemed to close the door for him.

"We watched Zack go through a difficult time," recalls his sister, Beth. "He felt forsaken by God. He seemed lost. He tried other things, but nothing motivated him like his childhood dream. I remember the day I asked him if he believed God had created him for a military career. He said, 'Yes, absolutely. It's all I've ever wanted.' So I told him if God had given him that lifelong desire, there had to be a way for him to pursue it."

Being reminded of the truth about who gave him his dream was enough to motivate Zack to try again. He called a recruiter who remembered him from the training program. The recruiter encouraged Zack to take the physical exam to see if he could pass the vision test. But Zack balked. He'd failed similar tests before.

"I encouraged him to go anyway," says Beth. "I said, 'If God created you to serve Him in uniform, He'll make a way even though there isn't a way at this moment.'"

And God did make a way. Zack passed the test. He's now serving in the marines, living the dream God created him for. And his sister witnessed the power of a reclaimed dream to shape a life.

When we set out each day as sent ones who know how important every person's big dream is and how many people are stuck or remain uncertain in this area, we place ourselves in very promising territory for miracles. It's a part of the Everyday Miracle Territory that our Creator cares passionately about, and we can expect Him to show up with power.

We are stepping out as volunteers with exceptionally good news. "You are not an accident. You are one of a kind. Your big dream is from God, and it's irreplaceable. And you were meant to seize it and celebrate it every day of your life!"

Let me show you what that might look like in your life.

Profile of a dream deliverer

Once a person claims the truth of the God-invented dream in every heart and learns a few simple skills, he takes on great influence with others. I've seen it many times, and perhaps you have too. With a little practice, you'll be able to recognize a need in this area and speak to it with authority and insight.

My friend Joe is like that. He grew up in a missionary family where pursuing the dream was a big deal. Joe says his dad used to tell him, "Son, you can grow apple trees or fly jets. If that's what you were born to do, then it's the Lord's work for you. And I promise you there's no unemployment in the Lord's work!"

These days Joe's home is a favorite hangout for college students. For some reason they feel comfortable sorting through their hopes and dreams with him. I think it's because Joe has become a dream champion. He helps others see that their life was always meant to matter—a lot!

A goal of this chapter is to empower you to be another Joe or Beth, a sent one who knows that everyone is born with a life dream from God and who is prepared to help them pursue it.

Don't worry—being a dream delivery person for God is *not* the same thing as being a career counselor. We need those too. But what we're aiming for here is to prepare you to deliver miracles of life direction and purpose in many lives through God-directed conversations. That miracle dimension— where God shows up through us for the benefit of others and for His glory— makes all the difference.

One of my favorite examples of this kind of God-directed conversation is found in the Bible story of Abigail's meeting with David, the future king of Israel. We first see her at a low point in David's life. David is about to commit murder, and the man he plans to kill is Abigail's husband. Just imagine how that one act could have severely sidetracked the dream that God had placed in David's heart.

Along with the rest of Israel, Abigail knows that David has already been chosen by God to be king. Since she knows God's dream for David, she takes an enormous risk of faith, setting out to intercept David before he can carry out his plan. When they meet, Abigail brings David a generous supply of food and something even more valuable—a timely reminder of his destiny.

You'll find her dramatic speech in 1 Samuel 25, but a paraphrase might read something like this: "David, God has not forgotten you. You will become king as He has promised. In the meantime, don't do something foolish like taking vengeance on my husband. That would only jeopardize what's really important—God's amazing dream for your life."

David's response to her is so telling. Right away he recognizes that she is a sent person. He says:

> Blessed is the LORD God of Israel, who sent you this day to meet me!
> And blessed is your advice and blessed are you, because you have kept
> me this day from coming to bloodshed and from avenging myself with
> my own hand.[4]

If you had asked David, "Did a miracle just happen here?" he would have said, "Absolutely!" He knew God had intervened—that the miracle was directly from God. Before Abigail showed up, he was dead set on the wrong direction. Then, out of nowhere, a stranger appeared and delivered a message that put his whole life in perspective. That changed everything. His anger evaporated. In its place came gratitude, acceptance, and new hope for his future. What had Abigail done? Really just one thing. She had reminded him of God's big dream for his life when he had lost sight of it.

I point you to Abigail's story because in your new life of inviting God to show up in miraculous ways, you are called to do the same thing—and you can.

Do you wonder how Abigail knew what to say? For example, did she pull out a written speech that she had tucked into her saddlebag? I don't think so. I think she invited a miracle and opened her mouth and depended on God's Spirit to fill it. Obviously, David recognized every word as coming to him straight from God.

In the same way, we can relax as sent persons. Once we ask to be sent and we care about championing God's big dream for others, He will bring people across our path that He knows we can help. When we align ourselves with what God wants done, He will help us. He will bring us divinely arranged encounters, and He will show up to deliver a miracle through us.

How to deliver a dream

Let's look at how the five-step delivery process applies to this new miracle key. As you would expect, you'll be able to apply much of what you've learned in the Money Key to this one too.

Step 1: Identify the person. You might be nudged by God or alerted by circumstances (as when Abigail realized that David was about to compromise his dream). But more than likely, you'll need to rely on cues and bumps to find the person God wants you to help.

If it's a cue, someone will say or do something that alerts you to the fact that he's struggling. You might pick up feelings of discontent, frustration, anger, or depression associated with how his life is going. You might notice an attitude of apathy or cynicism. These cues might be expressed in sentences you would have overlooked before:

- "My life is going nowhere. This isn't what I imagined for myself."
- "What I always wanted to do was…"
- "This job is the pits. I can't believe I'm stuck here."

Since people don't usually attribute their negative feelings to not living their big dream, you'll need to help them make the connection. My favorite clarifying bump in a dream context is this: "Are you living your dream, or are you stuck a little bit?"

It's informal, friendly, and positive, and it gets right to a big issue: most people think their big dream is out there somewhere, and they're just hoping it will come to them. That's where you come in. You know that their dream is closer to them than their own skin.

Did it strike you as odd in the Abigail and David story that a stranger could have so much influence on another person's dream? What I've learned is that people we don't know often have *more* influence in this area than those we do know. One reason is that those who are closest to us often can't see beyond the limits of our present experience any better than we can. I say this to encourage you to be willing to help anyone at any time to experience a dream breakthrough.

Step 2: Isolate the need. In my experience the vast majority of those you meet fall into one of two categories. Either they don't think they have a dream, or they are hindered from pursuing it in some way, usually by fear. And you can help both of these types of people.

For the one who doesn't think he has a dream, you now have a lot of truth to help you shape your questions. Do so conversationally. Keep your voice low, your statements personal and from the heart. You might start by saying, "You know, we all had a big dream when we were young. What was yours?" Or bring the conversation into the present: "If you had all the money and freedom you needed to pursue your big dream, what would your dream look like?"

You might learn that the other person stuffed his dream into a closet a long time ago. Or that he has never understood how important it is to pursue a God-given dream. With help from you and God's Spirit, he can have a breakthrough about what God wants—and what he wants too.

Ask those who know their dream, but feel stuck, to describe the dream. You'll find that many are afraid of what others might think or even of the dream itself. Some have never shared their heart on this matter with anyone. That's why revealing a dream to a receptive, nonjudgmental person can be such a powerful step forward. As they talk, ask God to show you what's holding them back.

The truth is, every dream from God *is* too big and too hard. That's why He gives us a lifetime to pursue it with His help. So the very fact that the person you're talking to feels afraid confirms that you are right on track. After all, we don't struggle with such fears when we stay in the same old rut or when we decide to do what everyone expects.

The fears each of us faces in pursuing a life dream tend to fall into two easy-to-remember categories:

- Fears about failure. The dream seems too big, or we feel disqualified to pursue it.
- Fears about rejection. The dream is opposed by others whose opinions we greatly value.

In my book *The Dream Giver*, I called these Comfort Zone fears and Border Bully fears. But the most important thing to do when you're isolating the need is to help others name their fears in their own words. You might ask, "If you were to describe the one biggest hindrance to your dream, what would you say?" You're going to find that simply helping a person put his finger on his fear is often enough to begin turning on the lights in his understanding. Let God guide your conversation. Now that you know the truth about big dreams, you're in the right place to invite a breakthrough for him by God's power and wisdom.

Once the fears are expressed, you're ready for the next step. Remember, isolating a need is different from solving a problem. You aren't a problem solver or life counselor. You are a planter of seeds of truth. You are a Heaven-sent dream champion.

Step 3: Open the heart. By this time you'll know if the person is open to thinking about his dream in a fresh way. When I think of opening a heart in the context of delivering a dream miracle, I imagine a single burning ember in a fire grate or campfire. My job is to find that ember, then get on my hands and knees and gently, persistently blow on it until it bursts into flame.

The ember is the person's big dream; your task is to reignite his desire for it. Here are some suggestions from my experience on how to do this with the people you meet.

Affirm that God does have a dream for them: "If you ask God to help you know your dream and discover your big purpose in life, He will help you find it."

Ask them to describe their dream and to describe what their life will be like when they are living it. Then ask them to describe what they are doing now. The comparison will increase their desire for the dream. You might say, "I've discovered that if I'm not pursuing my dream, my life just doesn't make much sense."

Help them see how important their dream is to God, and affirm its value for them. (That's what Abigail did for David.) They may feel embarrassed by it. More than likely, people close to them have dismissed it as impractical or impossible. So you might say, "I can see you doing that and really enjoying it. You'd be successful too."

Affirm their ability to live out their dream: "God wouldn't create you for a dream that isn't doable. It's impossible to do all of it at once, but if you keep moving in the right direction, you *will* see it happen. You just need to take the next step."

Ask them to go to the end of their life in their imagination, then look back: "What would make you really happy to have done with your life?" Or, "What do you think God would say to you if you've spent a lifetime really getting after the dream He gave you?" Or, "How would you feel if you came to the end of your life and discovered you hadn't done what you were created to do?"

To encourage them, ask them to tell about a time in the past when God was faithful and good to them. What does that suggest they can expect from Him in the future?

Challenge them with the truth: "Would you say, then, that God expects you to pursue your dream?" If they say yes, then ask, "What could be a next step to getting you back on track?"

Remember that we never speak into another person's heart from our head. Rather, we connect from our heart to theirs. People have many longings attached to their dreams, and if they're not pursuing them, they have much pain and regret. As an ambassador of Heaven, you can help them see God's passion for their dream.

If you want to see God's heart on display on this issue of a life dream, read Paul's second letter to the young pastor Timothy. Paul is writing about Timothy's calling to be a minister, but the sentiments and values apply directly to any life dream. You'll find emotionally charged, dream-reigniting words like "Stir up the gift of God which is in you," and "God has not given us a spirit of fear, but of power and of love and of a sound mind."[5]

> When a person is feeling stuck, his dream will seem small while his fear will seem overwhelming.

Paul knew that since you can't make someone's fear go away, the best thing to do is to build up his desire for the dream until it becomes stronger than his fear. When a person is feeling stuck, his dream will seem small while his fear will seem overwhelming. Our job is to set the forest on fire with his desire for his dream. And while we're doing our part, God will be at work on the inside, doing what only He can do.

Step 4: Deliver the miracle. Your precommitment to actively partner with the Spirit and to proactively exercise your faith in dependence on God are what prepare you for success in this step. Your part in a miracle is to prepare the person for the work of God; it is God's part to do the miracle. And remember how much God cares about the dream He put in each person's heart! While you encourage and inform, His Spirit will be at work in the person in numerous ways. He will take the seeds of truth you share and work in the person to bring about change. Without a change in belief, behavior cannot change. God stepping in here is the difference between your saying something helpful and a breakthrough that is miraculous.

We saw how God stepped into the life stories of Zack and David and the women at the Mary Hall Freedom House. Think of God's motivation to show up in that moment—to take a seed of encouragement and hover over it with His Spirit so that it flames up in their hearts and motivates them for years.

That's what we do. And that's what God does. Trust Him to do what you cannot do.

What does a dream miracle look like? You can always trace it to a change of belief—a paradigm shift—that results in the person's reaffirming his dream and acting on it in a way he couldn't before. For example:

- A person believes for the very first time that God does have a special and big purpose for his life and that he is precious and priceless.
- A person understands for the first time what his dream might look like.
- A person has a revelation about what is holding him back from beginning his dream.
- A person understands for the first time why he has felt stuck on the journey to his dream, and he resolves to step over or through the hindrance.
- A person who has abandoned his dream or hidden it away pulls it out of the closet, brushes it off, and moves forward in living his dream.

A miracle takes place by the Spirit moving in a heart. This doesn't mean our thoughts aren't involved; it just means that the miracle ultimately occurs in our heart and shows itself in our behavior. You'll know when it happens. The person's face will change. He may very well become emotional—dreams overflow with emotion and desire. He will seem lost in thought. By what he says next, you'll know that God has made His move.

Don't leave the conversation without leading the person to recommit to God to finish his dream. Perhaps you could say, "God loves you so much, and I believe He brought us together. His dream for you may look impossible right now, but if you walk toward it, God is going to help you. He created you so you could finish your dream. Will you commit right now to do that, whatever it takes?"

Step 5: Transfer the credit. Here's where you make sure the attention goes to the right person. The outcome you're looking for is David's exclamation to Abigail: "Blessed is the LORD God of Israel, who sent you this day to meet me!"

To direct the person heavenward, say something like this:

- "Do you sense that God was involved in our talk today?
- "I think God is up to something wonderful with you and your dream!"
- "There's no doubt about it—God is really behind the dream. He planted it in your heart. He will be with you as you achieve it with His power."

More miracles for the road

My hope for you is that, with each step along your life journey, you will treasure and fulfill your dream more and more, and you will ask God to use you in miraculous ways to lead others to do the same. May you be like Paul, who even in his later years was still pursuing God's dream for him with all his might. In his last letter he wrote:

> *I press on, that I may lay hold of that for which Christ Jesus has also laid hold of me.... One thing I do, forgetting those things which are behind*

*and reaching forward to those things which are ahead, I press toward the
goal for the prize of the upward call of God in Christ Jesus.*[6]

This is the liberating news we deliver to other dreamers God brings our
way: "Your dream matters—to you and to God.
If you find yourself sidetracked, start again. It's
never too late to fulfill your destiny. God still
wants your dream to come true!"

Be ready every day to invite a miracle into the
life of a fellow traveler. Now that you know how
to be a dream champion in other people's lives,
I'm confident God will bring a dreamer in need of
a miracle your way soon.

*This is the liberating
news we deliver to
other dreamers God
brings our way:
"Your dream
matters—to you
and to God."*

12

The Forgiveness Key

You were born to deliver miracles of forgiveness

*W*hat *if each morning* you walked out the door knowing you were carrying a miracle key that could release someone from prison?

As dramatic as that might sound, it is the promise of this chapter. I can't think of any area of the Everyday Miracle Territory with more promise for immediate personal change than what we're going to talk about in this chapter. One reason the potential is so great is that you and I are surrounded by sincere, law-abiding people who *are* those prisoners and don't even know it.

It was Christmas Day, and Darlene and Jessica and I were out delivering meals for a local inner-city mission, asking God to send us to the people of His choosing. Our first delivery was to a family of seven. We found the house at the end of a long gravel road, surrounded by junk and broken-down cars.

The mother and an adult daughter came out to greet us. As soon as the mom saw the seven meals we'd brought, she exclaimed, "We're so glad you came! We were praying someone would come." She told us that her husband had lost his job and was sick in bed. "We just don't have any food or money in the house."

No food on Christmas? None of us could miss such an obvious cue. Nudge. *This is the family...*

She invited us in to meet her family. Her name was Mary Ann; her daughter's, Tess. While Mary Ann was introducing us around, she began to weep.

"Are you okay?" Darlene asked. Somehow we'd expected our delivery to bring more joy than tears.

"My baby drowned in the pool in the house behind us!" she said.

We could hardly believe what we'd heard. Instantly our hearts broke for her. "I'm so, so sorry," Darlene said. "I can't imagine what you must be feeling."

At that Tess started to cry too. We asked how it had happened. The mom told us she'd gone to work in the afternoon even though she'd felt strongly she should stay home. But her husband had insisted that they needed the income. While she was at work, her plan for childcare at home unraveled. The older son stayed in his bedroom, preoccupied with his music. Then the baby-sitter fell asleep on the couch. With no one to keep an eye on them, the two younger children wandered outside, then into the neighbor's backyard. By the time their absence was noticed, the youngest had drowned in the neighbor's pool.

"My baby drowned!" Mary Ann sobbed. "She was only two years old!"

By now Darlene had her arm around the mom, and my daughter and I were praying that God would show us how to bring His healing to such a devastating Christmas.

And that's when the conversation took a surprising turn.

"When did this happen?" one of us asked.

Tess looked at us through her tears. "Eighteen years ago," she said.

We were stunned. Until that moment we'd assumed that the accident had happened recently, maybe within the past few days. For Mary Ann, that's how it felt. But she and her family had been carrying their unresolved pain for eighteen years.

"You've really been through a lot, haven't you?" I said quietly to Mary Ann. "We're here for you. Would it help to talk for a while?"

Over the next ten minutes we heard a tale of almost unbelievable woe. In the years since the accident, Mary Ann had blamed the baby-sitter, her older son, God for not intervening, her husband for pressuring her to go to work that day, and especially herself. All that blame and bitterness had poisoned their lives. The marriage began disintegrating. Their son became an alcoholic. Tess had recently lost custody of her child to the authorities. The mom kept punishing herself for what had happened, but that hadn't helped either.

"Your whole family has suffered deeply, haven't they?" I said.

"We haven't been the same since that day," said Tess. "My mother used to laugh and smile. But not anymore. Not for eighteen years."

I turned to Mary Ann. "Would you say you have been in torment?"

"Yes, I guess I would," she said, wiping her tears.

"Would you like that to stop?"

"Well, yes," she said. "But how could that happen? We can't get her back!"

"Maybe that's why God sent us here today," I said. "Not just to deliver these meals but to bring a much bigger miracle. God is ready to set you free—completely, right here on Christmas Day in your kitchen!"

And that's exactly what happened. I gently led Mary Ann through the steps of forgiveness that we'll look at together in this chapter. She had a lot of old business to clean up—bitterness, anger, self-hatred, vengeance. But she took every step. And so did Tess. When we parted, mother and daughter were free for the first time in eighteen years.

Is it really possible that a heart wound left untreated could cause that much devastation in one life, in the lives of a whole family? Is it possible that an act as simple as forgiveness could be prized so highly by God that He releases miracles when it happens? And could His primary method of delivering this magnificent miracle be through willing servants like you and me?

In this chapter you're going to encounter a miracle key that has almost unlimited power for good in our world. Like the other two Special Delivery Keys, it requires a deeper understanding of several important biblical truths.

I'm talking about the Forgiveness Key.

The Forgiveness Key unlocks a miracle of freedom for those who suffer as a result of unforgiveness. When God connects you with a person in need, you draw on powerful Bible insights and universal principles to lead that person to healing. As you partner with the Spirit, God works through you to bring about a miracle of forgiveness.

In the next few pages, I'll show you why wrong beliefs about forgiveness keep so many people stuck in unforgiveness. I'll show you how Heaven views those wrong beliefs and what right beliefs God uses to bring freedom. You'll identify the simple steps every prisoner needs to take to break free, and you'll learn your part in delivering the miracle.

I often hear that, next to the miracle of eternal life, the miracle of forgiveness is the most powerful and precious experience a person can have.

Why forgiveness can save a life

If we lived in a perfect world, no one would need to forgive. No one would injure another person. No one would be abused or treated unfairly. No one would sin.

But we don't live in that world. We live in a world where, despite our best efforts, we hurt even those we love. We injure others accidentally and sometimes intentionally. And others do the same to us. It happens between individuals, races, countries. Watch the news; the hurts have been piling up for centuries.

That's why forgiveness is such an important experience for all of us. Without it, we could drown in an ocean of regret, pain, anger, and bitterness.

But there's a catch: forgiveness is one of the most *un*natural responses in all of human nature. Think about it. Selfless giving is hard enough, but forgiving? That's like lavishing the best gift ever on the person who just robbed you!

Why should a mother forgive the drunk driver who killed her son? Or a husband forgive his wife for having an affair with his best friend? Or a teenager forgive the father who left when she was a baby and has never made an effort to see her since? Or a businessman forgive the partner who asked for his all, then betrayed his trust? At those times everything in us cries out for justice, retribution, fairness—*not* forgiveness.

We have to ask, though, what happens when we don't forgive? What happens to the hurt?

Picture it like this: You're walking along the seashore when you step on a piece of broken glass. Ouch! You limp back to your towel and try not to think about it. Later you limp around chasing a soccer ball. The next day you're out walking around your vegetable garden in your bare feet. The gash hurts, that's for sure. But won't it heal in time? You decide to ignore the pain.

You continue ignoring it. The wound becomes infected, and your foot swells. Walking is difficult, but you still try not to think about it. Infection spreads. You break out in a fever…

> *When we don't forgive, it's as if we have chosen to leave dirt in a gash. Healing can't happen.*

You get the picture. If you treat the wound with care—wash out the dirt, protect it from germs—your foot will heal. However the wound happened, God made your body to heal itself. But if you leave the wound unclean and untreated, infection sets in. The healing process is blocked.

God made our heart the same way. When we forgive after we've been hurt, the wound gets cleaned out, and the healing process can start. When we don't forgive, it's as if we have chosen to leave dirt in the gash. Healing can't happen, no matter how much we try not to think about it, no matter how much time passes. In fact, the more time that goes by, the more the destructive consequences spread.

I call it the Spiral of Unforgiveness—the descent into greater and greater misery that occurs when a person's heart wound is left untreated. The first level of pain is bitterness, which inevitably leads to resentment. Unaddressed resentment spirals into anger. Anger deepens into malice and then hatred. Eventually a person is consumed by vengeance. Vengeful people live with the overwhelming desire, not simply to see justice, but to injure those who injured them.

Once you learn to recognize the cues, you'll realize that the symptoms of unforgiveness are everywhere in our world. Often the signs of it are right on the surface. A man who was unjustly fired months ago walks back into his old workplace carrying a rifle. Or a family like Mary Ann's suffers for years from anger and harmful choices.

But sometimes the evidence is overlooked or misinterpreted.

I remember a confused young man who came to me for advice. He said he just couldn't seem to finish anything. "I've started and dropped out of so many colleges I've lost count. No matter what I do, I can't get my life together." He described his various attempts to find direction. "I thought maybe you could help me."

Actually, I thought I could. I asked, "So, how has your dad hurt you?"

"My dad?" He assumed I was changing the subject, but soon a painful story came spilling out. "I can never live up to my dad's expectations—he is a perfectionist!" he said. "I know he wants the best for me, but I've never once felt his approval. Anything I tried, he told me to try harder. Anything I did wasn't good enough. Since I left home, it's easier just to avoid him."

I helped him see that avoiding the problem wasn't going to make things better. I described the picture of the untreated wound. "Would you say your father has wounded you?" I asked.

"Yes. A lot," he said. His face and posture were changing. I could tell he was feeling the years of disappointment and rejection deeply.

"Are those wounds still there, still infected?"

"Yes."

We talked about how much a boy needs his father's affirmation as he's growing up. For a young man who's been injured by a rejecting, judgmental dad, decisions become difficult. Motivation dries up. He can't see who he is anymore or where he wants to go.

"You can begin to undo the damage right now," I told him. "But to do that, you have to forgive your dad. There's no other way. Are you ready to do that?"

He was tearful but ready. Taking the injuries one by one, I helped him to forgive. By the time we were done, he could say to me, "Before God, I have forgiven my dad of everything." He was a free man.

"Now will you help me with my future?" he asked with a smile.

"I just did," I said. I gave him my address. "If you want, in a few months send me a note. Tell me how you're doing."

A few months later he wrote: "All my old insecurity and indecision are gone. It's like something came into my head and blew out all that bad stuff." He had reconciled with his dad and was excited about his future.

I hope you're seeing the far-reaching power of forgiveness to reclaim our lives from the injuries of the past.

With the need for forgiveness being so great in our world, how important would you suppose forgiveness is to God? To help you discover that, I want to pull back the veil of Heaven again and show you God's perspective on the matter.

I think you will be amazed.

How important is forgiveness to God?

The Lord's Prayer models how we should approach the heavenly Father. In His prayer Jesus reveals several things we can ask God to do—grant us provision, protection, and deliverance, for example. But you'll find just one thing that *we* are to do.

Forgive.

> *Forgive us our debts,*
> *As we forgive our debtors.*[1]

Jesus is telling His followers, when you pray—amid all your praises and petitions—be sure to affirm to the Father this one thing: that you are doing what He does. You are forgiving those who are your debtors and don't deserve your pardon.

In case His listeners miss the point, Jesus follows the prayer with only one commentary, and it's also about forgiveness:

> *For if you forgive men their trespasses, your heavenly Father will also forgive you. But if you do not forgive men their trespasses, neither will your Father forgive your trespasses.*[2]

Now, Jesus can't be referring here to what theologians call "salvation forgiveness." (That happens in Heaven and can't be earned—it is the gift of God to all who believe in Jesus Christ and His work on the cross as full payment for their sins.) He's referring instead to the flow of God's pardon in our lives on earth.

But clearly the stakes are high, or Jesus wouldn't have included these words about forgiveness. If I forgive, God will forgive me. If I don't, Jesus says, "Neither will your Father forgive your trespasses." Jesus leaves no room for confusion.

So I understand why Peter tried later to get Jesus to narrow it down to something a little more practical. He asked:

Lord, how often shall my brother sin against me, and I forgive him?
Up to seven times?[3]

Peter must have thought he was being generous. My brother steals from me, and steals from me again, and again and again. How about up to seven times, Jesus? Wouldn't that be enough? Wouldn't forgiveness beyond that turn into a terrible mistake?

But Jesus said, in effect, "No, Peter. Forgive him without limit."

I do not say to you, up to seven times, but up to seventy times seven.[4]

How can any of us forgive somebody seventy times seven—or really, an unlimited number of times? Jesus' answer reveals the single most powerful motivation to forgive that you'll find as you deliver miracles to those locked behind prison bars of unforgiveness. That's why Jesus shares it—to give Peter the understanding necessary to actually forgive another person seventy times seven!

It's a story about a servant who gets deeply, hopelessly into debt to his king. To recoup his losses, the king decides he must sell the servant, along with his wife and children, into slavery. When the servant learns what's about to happen, he rushes to the king and falls on the floor, begging for more time.

Something about his servant pleading facedown on the floor melts the king's heart. Jesus says he is "moved with compassion."[5] On the spot the king makes a decision. He doesn't just give him more time. He forgives the servant of every debt, and the servant walks away a free man.

Can you imagine how that servant must have felt? One minute he's in disgrace, in crippling debt, and facing an awful fate. The next he's debt free.

But the servant doesn't take his king's compassion to heart. No sooner has he left the king's presence than he corners a friend who owes him lunch money. When the friend can't pay up, the servant has him thrown in jail until he pays back the entire debt.

Then the king gets wind of it. Burning with anger, he calls the servant into his presence and tells him:

> *"You wicked servant! I forgave you all that debt because you begged me. Should you not also have had compassion on your fellow servant, just as I had pity on you?" And his master was angry, and delivered him to the torturers until he should pay all that was due to him.*[6]

Another stunning turnaround! From a blessed, free man one minute to a tortured prisoner the next. And only one thing will stop the torment—when he pays back everything he owes.

Don't miss who the king (also called master) is in the story. He is God the Father. We know that because Jesus is telling the story in answer to Peter's question about how often Christ's followers should forgive. Listen to what Jesus says next as He drives home the most shocking reason to forgive in the entire Bible:

> *So My heavenly Father also will do to you if each of you, from his heart, does not forgive his brother his trespasses.*[7]

You want to know God's views on forgiveness? Jesus told us. God doesn't think of forgiveness as simply a nice idea or a mere suggestion. In fact, just like the king in Jesus' story, God gets angry when those He has forgiven everything refuse to forgive each other of comparative trifles.

And we now know that when we don't forgive, He *will* act. Jesus clearly revealed that when He said: "So My heavenly Father also will do to you."

What exactly will the Father do? He will deliver us "to the torturers." God the Father doesn't torment anyone Himself, but Jesus shows that He does turn people over to the painful consequences of their own unforgiveness.

For how long? Just as Jesus said—until from their heart they forgive others their trespasses.

Now you know why I asked Mary Ann that unusual question: "Would you say you have been in torment?" That simple question validates for you and me and everyone a deep need for a forgiveness miracle.

You want to know God's views on forgiveness? Jesus told us. God doesn't think of forgiveness as simply a nice idea or a mere suggestion.

Over many years of delivering this miracle, I've never had people with unforgiveness in their heart reply no when asked if they are experiencing torment. In your miracle appointment, God the Father wants the person to be released from the prison of torment. Not only has He sent you to deliver the miracle for Him, but His Spirit has been actively at work in the person's heart ever since the moment the wound occurred.

And what does God want most from your encounter with another person locked up by unforgiveness? Not more suffering, that's for sure. He grieves with every wounded person that the injuries occurred in the first place. What God has always deeply desired for the wounded person is a supernatural deliverance from the prison of unforgiveness.

Freedom from the past starts when we grasp how strongly God feels about unforgiveness and when we initiate conversations knowing how strongly He desires to set people free of its misery.

Five steps to the delivery of a forgiveness miracle

The delivery steps described here will train you to lead a person to break through to emotional freedom. The more you deliver this miracle, the more skilled you'll become.

Fortunately, you already know a lot. For example, you've already seen how Heaven partners with us to deliver miracles of many different kinds. And the five-step delivery process you encountered in chapter 9 applies directly and in sequence here.

Step 1: Identify the person. Sometimes a person will acknowledge right away that a grudge or broken relationship exists: "I don't speak to my mother anymore." Or you might notice that when a certain topic comes up, a person withdraws or becomes overly sensitive. You might notice displays of chronic anger. Or you might see more generalized attitudes that often cover up old wounds—attitudes like cynicism, defeatism, bitterness, judgmentalism, and distrust of relationships.

Any emotional wound that happened a long time ago but still comes up in conversation or stirs out-of-context or inappropriate emotion is usually a giveaway. That's what happened with Mary Ann. She was experiencing an eighteen-year-old injury as if it were part of her life in the present. Whenever I see patterns of self-destructive behavior, I start with the assumption that unforgiveness could be an underlying cause. Whenever I see a difficulty in forming close relationships or confusion about life direction, I take these as important cues as well.

In your conversation, use affirmations, observations, and leading questions. Remember, you don't know yet if you're talking with your miracle appointment. You're simply using open-ended bumps to bring clarity:

- "That issue doesn't seem like it's been resolved. Are you still feeling unhappiness or pain because of what happened?" (You're observing an area of potential need, bumping for a sign of suffering or torment.)
- "Tell me about your family growing up." (A general question in an area where most of us experience hurts—more on this in the next step.)

- "That's a difficult subject for you, isn't it?" (The unspoken invitation is for the other to confirm his need.)
- "Do you ever feel like some painful things that happened earlier in your life are still holding you back?" (You're looking for signs of a pattern, confirming a need for forgiveness.)

Once you have begun to sense needs in this area, go to the most important bump for a forgiveness miracle—what I call the Unforgiveness Validator: "Would you say that you experience torment from time to time?" Then be quiet until the person has had time to think and respond.

You may feel uncomfortable the first few times you ask this validating question, but when you watch God working in person after person to immediately confess that to be true, you'll relax.

Once you are confident that the person you're talking to is your miracle appointment, you're ready to transition your conversation to the next step.

Step 2: Isolate the need. Obviously, God wants *all* unforgiveness to be taken care of. But rarely can people cope with all their wounds at one time. Count on God to reveal where and with whom He wants the breakthrough to begin. To isolate the need or needs that God wants to address, aim to bring focus in three areas:

- who hurt the person the most (the offender)
- what the offender did (the wounds)
- which injuries are the most emotionally distressing (the starting place)

Once you have your focus, don't stray to additional incidents or people.

Your intention is for the person who needs the miracle to have a clear list of grievances to work from—if not on paper, then in his mind. A clear list is all-important for the miracle to be effectively delivered. That's because unforgiveness is linked to the specific trespasses that caused the injury, not only to the person who inflicted them.

Keep in mind that a huge percentage of our hurts occur in our key relationships—a spouse, parent, child, sibling, close friend, relative, or an acquaintance at work or church. Bump with questions like "Think back over your life. Who hurt you most?" or "Would you share with me how you were hurt the most?"

You're in this conversation for one reason: to serve the person as a heart-wound physician who can facilitate the miracle of forgiveness. Be careful to remain sensitive and nonjudgmental as you are representing the Lord to the person and dealing with hurtful and at times even shameful areas that the person may never have shared with anyone before.

I've found that when we're partnering with God in this area, His Spirit is extremely active. He will bring specifics to the person's mind. Listen for expressions like "I don't know where this came from, but…" and "I had forgotten this…" That is the Spirit at work.

Now that you know who hurt the person most and have listed the specific, most distressing wounds, you're ready for Step 3.

Step 3: Open the heart. Jesus made it clear that release from torment can be granted only when a person forgives another "from the heart." The purpose of the third step, then, is to prepare a person to be emotionally ready to forgive the offender—not from the mind, not from the will, but from the heart. For that to happen, we must put him emotionally in touch with his wounds.

People can say, "Yes, I know I should forgive." But that doesn't mean they're ready to do it. A person can acknowledge compelling facts: "Uncle Robert hurt me badly. I have been devastated ever since. It continues to mess up my life today." But we still need to help that person become emotionally ready to let go of the injury.

Let go of what, specifically? Well, of a deep desire for justice. Of the need to even the score or get revenge. Of all the other powerful, entangling emotions that go with unforgiveness. And those feelings, no matter how toxic, can seem to the injured party like a necessary part of his identity. Strangely, to let go of them may strike the person as a loss, not a gain.

At this point the most powerful way to serve those who are trying to forgive is to share the story of Matthew 18, including the shocking revelation that they will be in torment until they open their heart and forgive. You've seen some of the most important truths in this chapter: the personal cost of unforgiveness, God's strong feelings and clear commands on the matter, and the very real promise of a complete end to torment—of escape from prison—once forgiveness is granted. Share these with the person who needs a miracle.

Try to identify the wrong belief that is keeping the person stuck, and help him see the right belief. You can remember three important ones with three *J*'s:

- Jesus: "Jesus forgave you. You can choose to forgive others."
- Justice: "Vengeance belongs to God, not to you or me."
- Jailer: "You are your own jailer. Your torment won't end until you forgive. Then it will end immediately. You will be free. And that is what God wants for you."

Keep the conversation focused on the person who needs to forgive, not on the one who caused the injuries. Again, your aim is to bring him to a point of readiness to forgive. Look into his eyes as you talk. You'll be able to tell when he opens his heart. The cues that his heart is open will be obvious— emotions, facial expressions, tone of voice, and often tears.

Now the person is ready to experience the miracle of forgiving.

Step 4: Deliver the miracle. At this point the person is ready to forgive, but with so many conflicting and swirling emotions, he doesn't have a clear path forward. In fact, he may even honestly say, "I really want to, but I don't know if I can." You serve as the human bridge from his "want to forgive" to his "did forgive." The Spirit of God will be leading you in this very personal process.

You can start by simply saying, "I'd like to help you do this. Would you be comfortable just repeating the words after me?" (Forgiveness between people is expressed not in a prayer toward God but as a statement of forgiveness toward the offender.)

If he agrees, gently lead him in a natural conversation, helping him to name and then forgive specific wounds that come to mind or that he has mentioned already: "I forgive my dad for telling me I'd never amount to anything...for walking out on my mom and me...for never being around..."

In certain instances you may need to help the person with a few open-ended questions:

- "What else did your father do that hurt you?"
- "Is there anything else that comes to mind?"

You are trying to get to the pain of his wound. Be patient and thorough, gently encouraging him to get it all out—every kind of injury and every occasion—and then forgive each instance.

Don't hurry the person, and don't become uncomfortable with periods of silence, as it gives the Lord time to work. Remember, this miracle is God's to deliver. Don't worry that the person may forget to name some wounds. The Holy Spirit will be leading his thoughts to deal with the real injuries.

Of course you will expect the real pain to trigger emotions—tears, anger, anguish. That's good and natural. Your role is to be a patient, caring listener.

When the person seems to be finished, use the Forgiveness Test. Ask the person to repeat these words out loud:

Before God, I have completely forgiven _____ of every wound.

Then be quiet for a minute and see if God agrees. During those few seconds of silence, the person usually remembers something else. After each new round of forgiveness, try the Forgiveness Test again until nothing else surfaces. Then you know the forgiveness part of the miracle has been successfully delivered.

The torment ends when forgiveness has been genuinely granted. Expect the miracle to bring with it a sense of peace. If you notice it, bring it to the person's attention: "You look more peaceful already. Do you feel lighter inside?" Forgiveness is one of the most beautiful miracles you'll ever witness.

Step 5: Transfer the credit. Your final step is to help the recipient of the miracle focus on the One he has offended by not forgiving. I like to remind the person that God has been present in the conversation and that He is the healer of hearts and the terminator of all torment.

But to complete the full miracle of forgiveness for himself, he needs to receive God's full forgiveness. Remind him that God views unforgiveness as sin: "How do you think God felt about your unforgiveness and bitterness for all those years?" At this point the person's heart is so tender that he will easily admit God hasn't been pleased with his anger and bitterness. Often I continue the process of leading the person in short phrases he can repeat after me: "Dear God, I confess my sins of unforgiveness... I have held on to resentment, bitterness, hatred, and vengeance... I have offended You and broken Your heart... Please forgive me for not forgiving."

Forgiveness can release healing in surprising ways. One breakthrough is often the beginning of restoration in other relationships.

And now you have delivered two gifts: the person who brought injury has been forgiven, and a person who offended God by not forgiving has also been forgiven.

In my experience, forgiveness can release healing in surprising ways. For example, one breakthrough in forgiveness is often the beginning of breakthroughs and restoration in other relationships, including a person's relationship with God.

The man who came running

To close this chapter, I want to take you back to a scene from chapter 1. Remember Jack, the waiter and single dad? I told you about meeting him in a restaurant one fall evening in Colorado. On the way to work he'd told God he desperately needed a hundred dollars to cover an overdraft. Then, during dinner, God nudged me in a very unusual way to open my God Pocket and deliver the exact miracle he'd prayed for.

But the story didn't end there.

Our dinner group had parted for the evening, and I was walking to my car when I heard someone call out, "Wait!" It was Jack, and he was bounding across the parking lot toward me.

"I just have to thank you again," he said. "That's never happened to me before."

He was done for the night and obviously wanted to talk. I reminded him that the money wasn't mine; it belonged to God, and I was just the delivery person. But I could see that what Jack was really trying to grasp was more than the fact of the miraculous provision. It was what that event *meant* that had him shaking his head—what the miracle said to him about God, about the meaning of his life.

As we talked more about his family situation, I felt that God wanted me to go further, so I asked, "Is God chasing you, Jack?"

Without hesitating, he replied, "Yes, He is."

"What about?"

He didn't answer. I could tell he was still trying to pull the strands of meaning together. But I thought I might know. I asked, "Has your ex-wife remarried?"

"No," he said.

"Have you remarried?"

"No."

"Are either of you in love with someone else?"

"No."

"Might God want you to get back together?"

"Oh, that's impossible," he said sadly. "I've said some terrible things and done some terrible things. And she's said and done terrible things to me." He stared off toward the mountains. "It would just never work."

But I didn't think that at all. And now that you understand how God sets up our miracle appointments, I know you wouldn't have either if you had been there!

I pressed forward. "If all that was worked out between you, what would you do?" I asked.

"Well, I'd ask her to marry me."

"Would you like to forgive her right here in this parking lot?"

Jack looked startled. "But that's impossible," he said.

"No sir, it isn't," I said smiling. "It won't even take very long."

And it didn't. As I led him toward a forgiveness miracle, Jack's heart was so open that he was straining forward at almost every step. You know what? From the moment I'd seen him running toward me across the parking lot, I knew he would be.

When we were done, he said with relief and a lot of conviction, "I'll be on my knees asking her to marry me by December!"

For Jack that night, one miracle had triggered another and another—like dominos falling. Not only did God meet Jack's financial need and set him free from unforgiveness, but He also became visible to Jack as a personal and loving God who still had a good future for his life.

I hope that, after reading this chapter, you never again underestimate the power of forgiveness, the cost of unforgiveness, or the urgent need for a forgiveness miracle in almost everyone you meet.

People everywhere are in prison. God's heart is broken. And you and I have been given a key that brings freedom.

Epilogue

———————◦✦◦———————

Welcome to the Beginning

If you're like me, you love nothing better than coming to the end of a successful adventure—unless it's starting a new one. Now that you've reached the end of this book, the best news is that it's only the beginning of your new life in Everyday Miracle Territory.

My hope is that you are not the same person you were when you read the first page. *You Were Born for This* was never meant to be *about* something; it was meant to *create* something—an unforgettable turning point in your life. Some may debate the terminology in the book or take exception to my interpretations. But that doesn't bother me much. What would break my heart is if you saw the wide vista of supernatural opportunity where God is inviting you to live…and you turned away.

Heaven's agenda in our world and in our daily lives is so much grander than millions of Christ's followers ever realize. But you have seen behind the veil of Heaven!

How many Christians have you met who realize that the flow of daily personal miracles for people in need is limited not by God but by people?

How many have you met who know that God is always looking for volunteers for His miracle missions, always sending signals about what He's doing and what He wants to do through us?

How many do you know who realize that partnering with God to do His work by His power is always possible?

My mission has been to awaken you to the largest, most promising life possible in your walk with God. He is, after all, the one "who is able to do exceedingly abundantly above all that we ask or think, according to the power that works in us."[1]

> *My mission has been to awaken you to the largest, most promising life possible in your walk with God.*

Have you encountered Him and His dream for you in a fresh way in these pages? I hope so.

If you have, you should already be seeing your life in radically different ways. Take a moment to measure how much your new beliefs have changed as you read the following statements:

- I used to see *miracles* as spectacular events from long ago or experienced these days by only a few. Now I see that God does personal miracles on a regular basis through ordinary people who know how Heaven works and who make God's agenda their own.

- I used to see *other people* in terms of what they appeared to be on the outside. Now I recognize that every person is someone with a need—perhaps known only to God—that He deeply wants to meet, very possibly through me.

- I used to see *Heaven* as a place where I might live someday. Now I recognize that Heaven is also a place where God is busy right now planning miracle appointments on earth and looking for people who will volunteer to partner with Him in delivering them.

- I used to see *myself* as someone who might experience a miracle someday. Now I see that God is ready to do miracles through me regularly to meet important needs for others. (And I'm on Heaven's list of reliable miracle delivery agents.)

- I used to see a *world* in which I was powerless to change much. Now I see a world where every urgent need or painful lack brings to mind how God's desire from the start has been to work supernaturally to meet those needs through people like me.

- I used to perceive *God's Spirit* as a mysterious and invisible force that felt remote from my daily life. Now I see the Spirit as a Person who wants to partner with me in supernatural ways to accomplish Heaven's agenda.

- I used to assume that a *miracle appointment,* should I have one, would be shrouded in mystery and that my chances of success would be small. Now I realize that identifiable signals and delivery steps can lead me toward success in any miracle mission and that God wants me to succeed even more than I do.

- I used to see *today* as a day like any other day, when God probably wouldn't intervene in any noticeable way. Now I see every day as an exhilarating opportunity to be sent on a miracle mission to a person in need, and I can expect success because His power will work mightily—through me!

If you find yourself resonating with the truths of the second sentence in each statement, congratulations! You have taken the message of this book to heart. Now you know that partnering with God in His miracle agenda for others isn't just frosting on the spiritual cake—it *is* the cake.

Go through the roof

One of my favorite New Testament stories about delivering a personal miracle is the account in Luke of four friends who decided to bring a paralyzed man to Jesus for healing. Their timing couldn't have been worse. The house where Jesus was teaching was crammed with an overflow audience.

With every door and window blocked, how could the friends get the man on the stretcher to Jesus? They saw no possible way to make their miracle appointment. Should they turn back?

Luke tells what they decided to do instead:

> *When they could not find how they might bring him in, because of the crowd, they went up on the housetop and let him down with his bed through the tiling into the midst before Jesus.*[2]

That sentence reads so innocently, doesn't it? But imagine the scene…

First, a lot of stomping and shuffling on the roof.

Jesus pauses in midsentence. Some of the listeners glance up.

Then dirt and bits of tile start tumbling down as a hole opens above their heads. Now everyone is staring up in disbelief. The owner of the house is outraged, the guests aghast. They jump to their feet, shouting at the scoundrels on the roof to stop or else!

But the four men don't stop. The hole yawns wider. Then down comes a stretcher, lowered inch by inch with ropes. On the stretcher is a wretched shell of a man who comes to rest on the floor right in front of Jesus.

Everyone looks at Jesus. How will He react? If He's really God, *how will God react?*

And that's when they see that Jesus is still looking up toward the ceiling and into the faces of the four hopeful men.

How do I know that?

"When He saw their faith," the Bible says ("their" referring to the men on the roof), He turned to the paralyzed man on the mat and said, "Your sins are forgiven you.... Arise, take up your bed, and go to your house."

Immediately he rose up before them, took up what he had been lying on, and departed to his own house, glorifying God. And they [the crowd looking on] *were all amazed, and they glorified God.*[3]

From four friends with no opportunity...to mission accomplished and an unforgettable display of God's power and glory. How did that happen?

The answer is simple but not easy. When the friends couldn't see a way forward, they went forward anyway. They created a new way, refusing to be stopped by challenging circumstances. They also refused to be influenced by other people's expectations. Their desire to receive God's miracle for a friend was much greater than all that.

You Were Born for This is my best attempt to help you see that God can and will work through your faith to bring miracles to others. You don't need the perfect opportunity. You don't even need to be perfectly prepared. That's because you are already the perfect candidate to deliver a miracle.

Remember?

You are a *sent person* (Master Key) who *shares God's heart for people* (People Key) and who *intentionally partners with the Spirit* to do God's work (Spirit Key) through *acts of proactive dependence on Him* (Risk Key) to deliver His miracle to others.

So how does God see you right now? I think Jesus showed us. The same Lord who was passionate about delivering the gifts of Heaven to people in need is looking at you right now with pleasure and great anticipation.

Thoroughly equipped

What are some personal decisions you could make today that would ensure your new miracle life continues to flourish? I recommend five.

1. *Commit.* Are you ready to "go through the roof" to make your miracle deliveries? In every miracle opportunity you'll come to a point where you won't know the *how* of your next step. But that's when faith that pleases God makes a surprising choice. When you see no possible way to do what God wants done, you move forward anyway in confident dependence on Him. In my experience those are so often the situations that lead to the miracle stories I never tire of retelling. Commit now to pursuing your miracle opportunities, knowing that God will show up in supernatural ways.

> *When you see no possible way to do what God wants done, you move forward anyway in confident dependence on Him.*

And here's a small but powerful action I encourage you to take: sign in today with the growing online community at www.YouWereBornForThis.com. Why is this so important? I've noticed that two kinds of decisions rarely, if ever, result in life change: private decisions and postponed decisions. That's why publicly identifying and joining with others who share your new commitments has so much power.

2. *Act.* You can't master every principle in this book today, but you can ask to be sent to a person in need today. You can go through every conversation today newly awakened to what God might be bringing your way. You can respond to His nudge. You can watch for cues. You can bump. There's so much you already *can* do.

Which means that already *you can do your part* in the partnership with God. If you do yours, God will do His. You will find yourself standing in front of your miracle assignment with everything you need to know to cooperate with joy and success in a supernatural provision.

Ask God to show you what He's already prepared you to do. For example, your life experience, especially in an area where you've struggled or suffered, often suggests the kinds of people and situations where you will find the most opportunities. Ask God to bless you now with miracle delivery opportunities in the very areas where you have experienced pain in your past. Your life will have prepared you especially well for Step 3 of the delivery— "Open the heart."

Don't worry that God will ask you to do more than you're ready for, especially when you're just getting started. God loves beginners, and as you've seen, He perfectly matches each miracle opportunity with His best choice for the delivery agent.

3. *Grow.* Determine now that you will do whatever it takes to be ready for any miracle assignment God wants to send your way, even ones that seem completely out of reach to you now.

The most important way to grow your effectiveness is by studying the Bible for miracle ministry insights in addition to daily encouragement. God's Word has been given so that every delivery agent "may be complete, thoroughly equipped for every good work."[4] Since every miracle is a good work, think about the implications of that statement. *God has already made a way for you to be "thoroughly equipped" for every single miracle mission you were created for!*

The special delivery miracles presented in this book are just three that can and will happen when you apply biblical principles. Begin now to intentionally prepare for personal miracles in other areas such as troubled relationships, habitual sins, and a need for salvation, to name a few. And visit the book's Web site for Bible studies and other helpful resources for personal growth.

Another way to grow is to apply the basic principles and tools you're learning on a larger scale—in your family or another small group, for example, or even in bigger arenas in your community or around the world. Every principle or tool in the book works because it is based on how Heaven works. That means your miracle partnership with God has virtually no limit in where you can apply it for His glory. Take bold steps outside your comfort zone and watch what God will do.

4. *Multiply.* It is my deep desire and continual prayer that the truths in this book will liberate millions around the world to discover new ways of partnering with Heaven to serve the needs of humankind. But every movement starts with one person. So consider what you can do to multiply the message of the miracle life to others.

You know that Jesus commanded each of His followers to go and make disciples. But I'm always struck by what He didn't say. For example, He didn't command, "Go when you're ready" or, "Go if you're in professional ministry" or, "Go, but you don't have to make disciples if you just love people."

Here's the amazing truth: what Jesus commands you and me to do is nothing less than what God created us to do and will empower us to accomplish. When you make a priority of multiplying in the lives of others what God has given you, you'll find personal fulfillment and fruitfulness that you can't experience any other way.

Begin to multiply the message with the people God has already placed in your spheres of influence. Why not work your way through this book with your family? with your friends and co-workers? in your small group at church?

If you're a pastor, consider preaching through these topics to further equip your congregation to live in a miraculous partnership with the Spirit. Imagine what would happen in your community if the majority of your members learned how to depend on God's power for miraculous ministry results. Your church would be bursting at the seams with people who have witnessed what God can do through them and who can't wait to learn more.

Do you have a personal miracle story to tell as a result of reading this book? Go to www.YouWereBornForThis.com, click on "My Miracle Story," and share what happened. You'll encourage others and give God credit for what He's done. The Bible is full of stories of how God intervened in time and space and what happened in people's lives as a result. Now it's your turn to share.

And that brings me to a final step every miracle delivery agent should take.

Declaring His power

We live in an era that seems to have reduced much of the Christian life to two expectations: what God can do for us, and what we can do for God. But every page of this book has been intended to demonstrate to you a third and profoundly more thrilling expectation: what God can do through us for others.

And this brings me to my final encouragement to you.

5. *Declare.* Have you noticed how much of the Bible is devoted to recounting God's wonders? Scores of the psalms and major portions of both Old Testament and New retell God's miraculous deeds for all to hear. But in our generation, the wonders that God has done and will continue to do for us and through us are so often overlooked.

> *Will you join in reclaiming for our generation the reputation of our miracle-working God?*

"One generation shall praise Your works to another," wrote the psalmist, "and shall declare Your mighty acts.... Men shall speak of the might of Your awesome acts, and I will declare Your greatness."[5]

Will you join in reclaiming for our generation the reputation of our miracle-working God? Will you reclaim for yourself and those you love your birthright to the miraculous as a normal way of life?

You and I were born for this...even if we have to go through the roof to do it.

Acknowledgments

No project of this magnitude could have come together without a lot of help, and I've been blessed to receive it from so many. Because of the unusual nature of the topic, I tested the material before a wide range of ten different audiences, including churches of many stripes and an internationally representative gathering of ministry leaders in Hong Kong. On each occasion, audiences contributed valuable insights, and to all of you I am grateful. In particular I am thankful to those who attended a four-week teaching series organized by Bruce and Toni Hebel in Tyrone, Georgia. Your meaningful engagement with the content and your eagerness to put it into action have been a source of tremendous help and encouragement.

The publishing executives at WaterBrook Multnomah and the Crown Publishing Group have gone to extraordinary lengths to ensure the success of this project. I am grateful to Stephen Cobb, Ken Petersen, Carie Freimuth, and Lori Addicott in Colorado Springs and to Jenny Frost, Michael Palgon, and David Drake in New York City. Your enthusiasm and support, both personally and professionally, have been indispensable, and I do not take it for granted. Thank you.

The closer a book comes to a daunting deadline, the more authors require the skill and patience of the editorial and production teams. To Julia Wallace, managing editor; Laura Barker, editorial director; Mark Ford, senior art director; Kristopher Orr, graphic designer; Carol Bartley, production editor; Karen Sherry, interior designer; and Angie Messinger, typesetter—thank you for your perseverance and good cheer.

I'm already impressed by the creativity and energy of the marketing team at WaterBrook Multnomah and look forward to partnering with you for many successes in the future. To Tiffany Walker, marketing director; Allison O'Hara, marketing coordinator; Melissa Sturgis, senior publicist; and Chris Sigfrids, online marketing manager; and to all those who work with you—thank you so much.

It's been a pleasure to work again with David Kopp as my writing collaborator, and his wife, Heather Kopp, as our editor. Both of you have contributed extraordinarily to the vision and substance of this book. I am truly blessed by your abilities, creativity, and tenacity, and I'm grateful for your friendship. Thank you.

From early in the writing process, the writing team benefited greatly from the clear thinking and careful work of Eric Stanford, an informed reader and a superb line editor. Many thanks.

I owe more than I can say to my executive assistant, Jill Milligan, with whom I've worked closely for more than thirty years. As always, your enthusiasm and organizational talents turn impossible challenges into accomplished goals in record time. Thank you.

Finally, I express my deepest appreciation and affection to members of my family. First to my wife and closest partner, Darlene. Once again you supported, encouraged, and prayed me through to the finish. No man could ask for more than you are. And then to my daughters: Jennifer, your numerous insights and helpful reading of the manuscript helped shape the final product. Jessica, the weeks you invested as our editorial assistant brought great value to the book and treasured memories to your father. My deepest love and gratitude to each of you.

Atlanta, Georgia
July 2009

15 Frequently Asked Questions About the Miracle Life

For answers and other resources, go to www.YouWereBornForThis.com

1. I've seen so few miracles in my lifetime. Are you saying it's in my power to change that?
2. Don't I need a special anointing or gifting from God to deliver miracles?
3. Bizarre things seem connected with some people who claim to do miracles. Could you suggest some cautions that would help me stay balanced and on track if I go down this road?
4. I've really blown it in the past, and I'm still not where I'd like to be with God. Am I a candidate to partner with Him for miracles?
5. What happens if I fail to deliver a miracle or someone turns away?
6. People say "God told me" and "God led me," but I don't have those experiences in my spiritual life. Is something wrong with me?
7. After reading about the risk of faith, I realize I suffer from a lot of unbelief. Any suggestions for what I should do about it?
8. Couldn't people go overboard on nudges and prompts and end up making foolish decisions? How can I tell if a thought is from God or me?
9. The five steps of miracle delivery are helpful, but could you tell me more about that all-important fourth step: deliver the miracle?
10. Are there more keys to a life of miracles beyond what you've included in the book, or would you say this is the whole picture?
11. How can I be sure people will use my God Pocket funds in the right way?
12. So many are afraid to pursue their big life dream. Any more advice on how to help them overcome fear and take the next step in their journey?
13. Why do you say everyone needs a forgiveness miracle of some kind?
14. How could things change in our world if more people partnered with God in the supernatural realm? What could happen in churches?
15. I really want to learn more about delivery miracles. Do you offer other training materials, or could you recommend other helpful resources?

Notes

Chapter 1

1. 1 Chronicles 4:9–10
2. *Merriam-Webster's Collegiate Dictionary*, 11th ed., s.v. "miracle."

Chapter 2

1. Acts 1:4
2. Acts 1:8
3. 1 Corinthians 2:1, 3–5
4. Ephesians 2:10
5. Ephesians 1:17–20

Chapter 3

1. 1 Kings 22:19–22, adapted
2. 1 Kings 22:22
3. 1 Kings 22:34–37
4. John 5:17, NIV, adapted
5. John 5:19–20
6. 2 Chronicles 16:9

Chapter 4

1. John 20:21; Mark 16:15
2. Isaiah 6:1–4
3. Isaiah 6:8
4. James 5:16, emphasis added

Chapter 5

1. 1 Peter 2:9
2. Luke 22:27; Matthew 20:28; John 6:38
3. Jonah 3:1–3
4. Jonah 4:1
5. Romans 5:8
6. Colossians 3:23–24

7. Matthew 25:40

8. Matthew 25:40

9. See Jonah 4:11

Chapter 6

1. John 16:7

2. See John 16:7 (KJV), 13–14 (NKJV)

3. John 16:8

4. Acts 3:6, 12

5. 1 Corinthians 2:10

6. John 16:13

7. Psalm 32:8

8. Romans 8:14; Acts 18:5; 16:6

9. See John 16:8–14

10. Acts 4:13

11. See Luke 24:49; Acts 2:1–2

Chapter 7

1. Matthew 17:20

2. Matthew 13:58

3. Matthew 14:27

4. Matthew 14:28–29

5. Matthew 14:33

6. Matthew 14:30–31

7. Mark 6:6

8. 2 Thessalonians 1:11, NIV, adapted

Chapter 8

1. Isaiah 30:21

2. See 2 Kings 2:9; 4:2

3. Acts 8:39

Chapter 9

1. James 2:15–16

2. Luke 12:12

3. Luke 17:15–16

Chapter 10

1. 1 Timothy 6:18
2. Proverbs 19:17, ESV
3. Proverbs 19:17
4. See Mark 9:41
5. See Luke 21:1–4
6. Exodus 34:6
7. Matthew 5:16
8. Luke 14:13–14, NIV
9. See my book *A Life God Rewards* for much more on this topic.

Chapter 11

1. Jeremiah 1:4–5
2. Psalm 139:15–16
3. Ephesians 2:10
4. 1 Samuel 25:32–33
5. 2 Timothy 1:6–7
6. Philippians 3:12–14

Chapter 12

1. Matthew 6:12
2. Matthew 6:14–15
3. Matthew 18:21
4. Matthew 18:22
5. Matthew 18:27
6. Matthew 18:32–34
7. Matthew 18:35

Epilogue

1. Ephesians 3:20
2. Luke 5:19
3. Luke 5:20, 24–26
4. 2 Timothy 3:17
5. Psalm 145:4, 6

About the Authors

One of the world's foremost Christian teachers, **Bruce Wilkinson** is best known as the author of the *New York Times* #1 bestseller *The Prayer of Jabez*. He is also the author of several other bestsellers, including *A Life God Rewards, Secrets of the Vine,* and *The Dream Giver.* Over the past three decades, Wilkinson has founded numerous global initiatives. He has developed a Bible teaching faculty of over thirty-two thousand in eighty-three nations, led a movement of eighty-seven organizations that recruited and trained seven thousand Americans to serve the former Soviet Union, published ten monthly magazines, developed numerous courses that have been taught in more than ten thousand seminars, and led thirty-six hundred Americans to address hunger, orphan care, AIDS education, and poverty in Africa. Bruce and his wife, Darlene, have three children and several grandchildren. They live outside Atlanta.

David Kopp has collaborated with Bruce Wilkinson on more than a dozen bestselling books, including *The Prayer of Jabez*. He is an editor and writer living in Colorado.

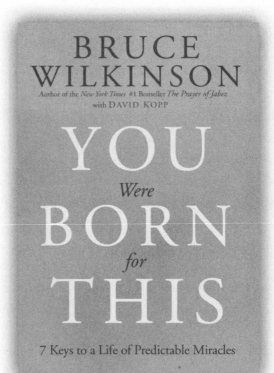

BRUCE
WILKINSON

Author of the *New York Times* #1 Bestseller *The Prayer of Jabez*
with DAVID KOPP

YOU
Were
BORN
for
THIS

7 Keys to a Life of Predictable Miracles

Available as an unabridged compact disc.

• Read by the author

• 6 CDs, 7 hours

RANDOM HOUSE
AUDIO PUBLISHING GROUP

Randomhouse.com/audio

Also available as an audio download.

Timeless Teaching
from Bruce Wilkinson

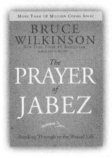

Learn the secret of receiving extraordinary favor, power and protection through a remarkable prayer.

Journey through John 15 and find three surprising secrets to achieving your unrealized potential through Jesus—starting today!

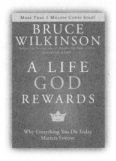

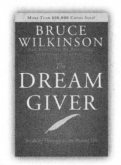

Bruce Wilkinson unveils God's plan to reward people in eternity based on the choices they make today.

Rise above the ordinary, conquer your fears, and overcome obstacles that keep you from living your dreams.

Additional information and resources available at BruceWilkinson.com.

Connect with Bruce online

To find out more about Bruce Wilkinson,
his books, and events, visit the website.

- Watch Bruce on video
- Share your life change stories
- Find upcoming events
- Get resources to deepen your faith

www.BruceWilkinson.com
www.YouWereBornForThis.com
www.Facebook.com/LastingLifeChange